FULFILLMENT OF PURPOSE

Volume Two

Writings by Marie S. Watts

The Ultimate

Prayers and Excerpts from The Word

Success Is Normal, Just Be Yourself,
   Your Eternal Identity

Fulfillment of Purpose, Volume One

Fulfillment of Purpose, Volume Two

You Are the Splendor

Gems & Poems of The Ultimate

The Gospel According to Thomas

Three Essential Steps

The Omnipresent I AM, Volume One

The Omnipresent I AM, Evidenced, Volume Two

The Ultimate Awareness, an Eternal Constant,
   Volume One

The Ultimate Awareness, an Eternal Constant,
   Volume Two

These and other books available through:
Mystics of the World
Eliot, Maine
www.mysticsoftheworld.com

FULFILLMENT OF PURPOSE

Volume Two

Marie S. Watts

Fulfillment of Purpose

Volume Two

by Marie S. Watts

Mystics of the World First Edition 2015
Published by Mystics of the World
ISBN-13: 978-0692543245
ISBN-10: 0692543244

For information contact:
Mystics of the World
Eliot, Maine
www.mysticsoftheworld.com

Photography by © Dr. Joel Murphy 2015
www.DrJMphotography.zenfolio.com
Printed by CreateSpace
Available from Mystics of the World and Amazon.com

ৎ ৩

CONTENTS

Introduction

Dear Reader:

These two volumes of classwork, entitled *Fulfillment of Purpose*, are being presented as the fulfillment of a definite purpose. The basis of this work is the Absolute Ultimate, and it is being written solely for those who have transcended the duality of metaphysics and have discovered that the Absolute is the only way for them. "God is All, All is God" is, of necessity, our *only* basis.

Sometimes it appears that we experience a period of uncertainty after we have left the methods—affirmations and denials—of metaphysics. No longer can we do "mental work." Yet we realize that our Consciousness must be purposefully active. We know that we cannot completely ignore the seeming problems that appear to present themselves. Neither can we accept these illusions as though they were genuine. Always these questions arise: "If I cannot do anything about these illusory problems, what should I do? What should the activity of my Consciousness be? How am I going to perceive and manifest the Perfection I know to be All?"

We are aware of the fact that we cannot *use* the Absolute. Thus, there can be no method, and sometimes it seems that we drift aimlessly and without purpose. Consequently, we often discover that our awareness of the Absolute does not seem to be evidenced in our daily affairs. In short, although we experience the sheer joy of knowing the Absolute, it may appear that we continue to be faced with problems.

There is a right way to contemplate, and this "right way" does not involve any assumptive thinking or reasoning so-called mind. Rather, it is the effortless way of simply perceiving the eternal, perfect, omniactive, omnipresent Omnipresence—God—which comprises the boundless Entirety that we call this Universe. In this right contemplation, the Absolute Truths we know are manifested in our daily affairs. Furthermore, in this right contemplation, we find that the Body does evidence the Absolute Perfection we perceive. This contemplation does not involve a method. Yet it is orderly, even as the activity of the Universe is orderly, and wonderfully simple when understood.

The purpose of this classwork is to reveal the orderly, specific way in which our contemplation fulfills its purpose. Knowledge is power. And the Mind that *knows* the way of purposeful contemplation is the Power that fulfills the purpose of this contemplation. In this way, the complete power of our "knowing" is realized, and it is evidenced in and *as* our daily affairs. Furthermore, this purposeful contemplation is manifested as the perfect Essence and Activity which comprises the Body.

In the first volume of *Fulfillment of Purpose*, we presented the universal fact of purposeful Existence.

In the second volume of this classwork, this universal, purposeful, omniactive Omnipresence is specifically revealed as our daily affairs, our homes, businesses, and as all our experiences. But this perfect, joyous, free, effortless fulfillment of purpose is also revealed as the Essence and the Activity of the Body.

It is imperative to inform you, dear reader, that the first volume of classwork should be thoroughly studied and contemplated before beginning the study of the second volume. The first book is a thorough preparation for this second volume, which is very specific in its revelations. Knowing the presence of the Power of the revelations herein set forth, I now lovingly dedicate this classwork to you, the beloved, enlightened reader.

Boundless Light and Love,
Marie S. Watts

Chapter I

The Practical Ultimate Absolute

The way of the sincere student of metaphysics is ever upward and onward. Ultimately he must arrive at the standpoint of the Absolute Truth. When this takes place, a tremendous upsurge of spiritual awareness is experienced. Once he perceives the Truth from the more expansive viewpoint of the Absolute, he realizes that he cannot return—or turn back—to the duality of metaphysics.

If the basic Absolute Truth, "God is All, All is God" is clearly perceived, it is virtually impossible for him to ever return to the contradictions and limitations of dualism. Inherently he knows that *this is the way*, and indeed he senses that somehow he has *always* known that Existence was—and is—the way it is revealed to be as the Absolute.

Again and again, you will hear him say, "Somehow I have always felt it was this way. I feel as though at last I have come home." And indeed, this revelation of the Absolute does seem like a glorious and joyous homecoming. This is true because the student has arrived at the recognition of his genuine and only Self; and of course, this revelation has been the basis of his seeming search all the while. Actually, though, it has been the God-Self insisting upon revealing and evidencing Itself as his Self that has kept him apparently searching.

It has been said that the Absolute does not heal or solve our problems. In a paradoxical sense this is true. Yet the Absolute does something far greater than healing or the solving of problems. It reveals the fact that there is nothing in need of healing and there are no problems to be solved. Furthermore, the Absolute does evidence Its Truth by being apparent as that which the world of appearance calls healing or the solution of problems.

The Ultimate Absolute is a purposeful Truth. In the study and contemplation of this Truth, we do not drift aimlessly around in a sort of rosy-hued cloud. Neither do we descend into the dualism of "mental work" or of "affirmations and denials." We no longer accept the "mind and idea" approach. Hence, our entire approach, in order to be purposeful, must be from a completely new standpoint. But this approach *must* be divinely intelligent.

The title of our textbook is *The Ultimate*. Thus, we have entitled our particular way the Absolute Ultimate or the Ultimate Absolute; and it is this very intelligent—yet entirely Absolute—way that evidences its rightness in perfect, joyous Being and Body. It is in the Ultimate Absolute that we perceive and experience being the evidence of Joy, Peace, Completeness, Perfection—and a glorious fulfillment of purpose.

In the first volume of *Fulfillment of Purpose*, we presented the way in which this perfect evidence of omnipresent Perfection is realized and evidenced as the Universal Truth. It is certainly important for you to have studied and contemplated the Truths revealed in the first volume before beginning the study of this second book. It is necessary to have a thorough understanding of the Truths presented in the first book, if this volume is to completely fulfill its purpose in and *as* your daily experience, your entire Being and Body. You see, within these pages you will perceive just how this Truth functions as your own Consciousness in every facet or aspect of your everyday affairs—your home, business, professsion, employment, and as the perfection of your Body.

Never do we begin our contemplation with the specific, sometimes called infinitesimal, and try to expand to the Universal, sometimes called the Infinite. Rather, our first approach is *always* from the standpoint of the Universe. This universal approach instantly disposes of the little assumptive person and dissolves all concern for any seemingly personal affairs or bodies. The so-called little "I" disappears in the contemplation of the infinite, or universal, *I*. Since it is the assumptive little "I" that appears to have or to cause all the trouble, the sooner we can become unaware of this little pretense, which is nothing, the sooner we perceive the glorious, complete Identity that we genuinely and eternally are.

But there is another wonderful factor that is so helpful in approaching every contemplation from the standpoint of the Universe: *there is infinite power in our seeing when we are perceiving from this limitless standpoint.* In fact, when we contemplate from this boundless, immeasurable standpoint, the whole power of the Universe is actively engaged in and *as* our contemplation.

Those who approach contemplation from the Universal standpoint but who do not follow this contemplation by being *specific* in their perception, may very well fall short of the realization and the evidence of the Truth of their contemplation. This is true because no matter what Truth we perceive as we are contemplating, this Truth is equally a universal and a specific Truth. Furthermore, there can be no separation between the Universal and the specific Truth, for they are *one and the same Truth.* If our daily lives and our Bodies are not evidencing the Truths we perceive in contemplation, it is because we have not contemplated from the specific, as well as from the Universal, standpoint.

It is true that each one of us is the indivisible, boundless, immeasurable, omnipresent All. Yet it is also true that each one of us is a distinct Identity. We must be very alert when we use the words *specific* or *distinct.* It is important for us to realize that neither of these words means division or separateness. There is distinction, but there is no separation in or as the one inseparable Identity, even though this Identity exists as the specific or distinct Identity that is evidenced as each one of us. The evidence of the

Truth we perceive is experienced and revealed within and as the Body of the specific Identity and in his daily living.

In this volume of *Fulfillment of Purpose*, our concern is mainly with the *evidence* of the Absolute Truth in and as the daily experience and the Body of the specific Identity. As we have stated before, you are a universal Identity. However, your attention is focused specifically in or as this distinct aspect of your Being, which is manifested as your everyday living and your distinct Body. Therefore, it is right here and now, as this specific aspect of your Being, that the Truth you know must be experienced and evidenced. It is in this way that the Universal Purpose is fulfilled, and it is in this way that your specific purpose in being *you* is fulfilled.

Of course, it does appear that our everyday affairs, business, or professional activity and our activity in the home are merely human activities and that we are functioning in a material world. It also appears that our associates and our families are separate human beings and that we work with—and are surrounded by—material objects.

This is the way it *seems*. But this is not the way it is. This, right here where our attention is focused at the moment, is not a material world. It is the very Kingdom—Consciousness—that is God, right here and now, and *You are this Consciousness*. This everyday living that seems to be human activity, having to do with separate human beings and material objects, is

15

not merely a human existence. Our associates and families are not temporary, separate humans. Neither are the houses in which we live, or the seemingly material objects of our home, or our daily experience really material in their essence or their activity. The foregoing may sound very unrealistic, but it is Absolute Truth, and we will discover how it is and why it is that this is true.

Behind and beyond every so-called human activity, there is genuine Universal activity, and this Universal activity is going on right where and when that which seems to be human activity appears to be taking place.

In like manner, wherever there appears to be a separate human being, there really is Spirit—Consciousness—*being,* and Consciousness is indivisible. Nonetheless, the specific Identity does exist, and there is a purpose being fulfilled as his existence. This is both universal and specific. It is impossible to separate the *universal* fulfillment of purpose from the *specific* fulfillment of purpose.

One might just as well imagine that the activity of the ocean was separate from the activity of the wave; that the activity of the wave was separate from the activity of the water or the drops of water. There is no separation, either of the activities or of the Identities who are engaged in the activities.

It is imperative that this inseparability be thoroughly understood. Otherwise, it will appear that we are speaking and acting dually. We are Absolute.

We speak and act as the Absolute Ultimate. We are the universal, indivisible, omniactive All, engaged in purposeful activity.

Often someone will say:

> Oh, I see the Truth so clearly and *know* it to be true in my morning contemplation, but when I go about my human activities in the home, the business, or whatever, it appears that I am in another world, and I forget all the beautiful Truths that I have known while in contemplation. Why is this true?

The answer to this paradox is really very simple. Yet it reveals a great basic Principle of the Ultimate Absolute.

The Consciousness that actively contemplates and the Consciousness that goes about the daily activities is the very same Consciousness. There is no way to separate Consciousness into periods of non-existent time, even as there is no way to separate Consciousness into areas of so-called space. The perfect, conscious Mind that contemplates is identically the same perfect, conscious Mind that performs every act in your home, your business, or any activity.

You do not become another Consciousness when your daily routine begins. Furthermore, your activity does not become a merely human activity in a world of illusion. You cannot separate the activity of the Mind engaged in contemplation from the activity of the Mind in and as your daily affairs. It is true that there are distinct *aspects* of the Mind in action, but the omniactive Mind remains forever the very same perfect Mind. The Truths you perceive in contemplation are just as present and equally active as your Mind, whether you are contemplating or whether you are engaged in the performance of your home duties, your business or professional experience, or your employment.

To imagine that you are one Mind in contemplation and another mind when you are engaged in business or home affairs is tantamount to being deluded by the illusion that you are two identities, with two separate minds. This, of course, is dualism, and really it is one of the most subtle aspects of dualism. You can "see through" this miasma when you realize that the perfect, conscious Mind you are when in contemplation remains identically the same perfect, conscious Mind you are during your daily activities. Furthermore, if you perceive this great Truth, you will find your daily affairs are conducted intelligently, smoothly, and effortlessly.

There is another aspect of this Truth that we should realize: that which we have called human activity really is divine activity. There is no such thing as human activity that can be separate from or other than the divine activity. This is why students of the Ultimate arrive at the point of effortless activity. All of their daily affairs just move smoothly and effortlessly, and there is no worry, no anxiety, no indecision, and certainly no struggle at all.

Please be assured that there are many students of the Ultimate who know this to be true because they are experiencing the proof of this Truth every day. Therefore, the foregoing statements are far more than just a beautiful theory. Rather, every Truth we have stated may be experienced by anyone who is completely aware of being the one inseparable Mind, Consciousness, Life, Love. We must realize that we cannot separate Mind into minds, Consciousness into consciousnesses, Life into lives, and Love into loves. When the perception of the indivisibility of the one and *only* living, conscious, loving Mind is clear, the Identity does live in perfect peace, joy, health, wholeness throughout every experience of his daily existence. There is no other way to experience the evidence of this Truth. The way of inseparable, infinite Oneness is the one and only way.

Now, we have stated that in this second volume of *Fulfillment of Purpose* we were going to discover the way in which this Truth functions as every aspect of our daily experience. Therefore, let us get on with this important aspect of our presentation.

First of all, let us begin with the Kingdom of God, in which you live and move and have your Being. Rightly understood, the word *Kingdom* means Consciousness. The Kingdom of God is right here, right now, because this glorious Kingdom is *your* Consciousness. In this Kingdom is the awareness of complete Absolute Perfection because it is God being aware as your Consciousness, and it is the Identity that you are, being aware as the Consciousness that is God. Thus, you are the Kingdom—Consciousness—that is God.

Furthermore, God—the Consciousness that you are—is the King of this Kingdom. This means:

> You are the Presence of the Power of Perfection in and as every act of your daily existence, and you are the Power of the Presence of Perfection in, and as, every event of your daily affairs.

Of course, this does not mean that you are a power *over* anyone or anything. Rather, it means that you are the *Power* of the Presence that comprises your experience.

In our book entitled *The Three Essential Steps*, we read, "Your Consciousness is your Universe." No greater statement of Truth could be revealed. Indeed, your Consciousness *is* your Universe, and conversely, your Universe consists of the Consciousness you are. Hence, only that which exists as your own Consciousness can be, or can be active, in and as your Universe.

Since your Consciousness is the Kingdom of God, your Universe—thus, your daily experience—is completely comprised of the activity of the living, loving, conscious Mind which is God. This, of course, is Mind purposefully active. Furthermore, it is Mind intelligently active. But above all, it is perfect Mind perfectly fulfilling Its purpose in being the Mind you are and the activity of the Mind you are. This being true, there can be no mistakes, no indecision, no failure, no friction, no strife, struggle, or effort. You see, Absolute Perfection is all that is — or can be — known by the ever-perfect, conscious Mind that you are; and perfect activity must, of necessity, be the only activity that is known as the perfect, conscious Mind that you are.

Now it is clear how it is, and why it is, that you are in the Kingdom of God right now and that you *are* the King *being* the Kingdom. You can also perceive that there is no difference between Heaven and Earth. Heaven *is* Earth when we really know that which comprises Earth. So-called human activities are divine activities when we rightly perceive the genuine Nature of the Consciousness that acts.

Jesus well knew the Truth of the foregoing statements. In the Lord's prayer he says, "Thy kingdom come. Thy will be done, as in heaven, so in earth" (Luke 11:2). There is tremendous significance in this statement of Truth, and as is the case with so many of Jesus' wonderful statements, this glorious, spiritual significance is overlooked. Jesus knew — and knows — that Heaven and Earth are the same and that the I AM God-Consciousness that *you* are is the Kingdom of Heaven eternally established as your everyday Life and that your activity is the activity of the King — God-Consciousness — that *you are.*

Beloved, your very awareness that you exist is the Kingdom of heaven, which is evidenced right here and now as your home, your business or

21

profession, your employment, or whatever activity you experience at any moment. Knowing this fact, you must, of necessity, perceive and experience the *evidence* of absolute harmony, perfection, joy, and peace in and as every aspect of your everyday affairs.

You cannot be active in any aspect of your Existence without being conscious of this activity. Consciousness is Awareness. Your awareness of the activity is your Consciousness being active *as* this activity. There is no inactive Consciousness. All activity is the purposeful Consciousness you are, constantly, perfectly, fulfilling Its purpose in being active. This is the Consciousness that you are when you are maintaining your home, when you are conducting your business affairs, when you are performing professionally, or when you are working at whatever your employment may be.

True it is that your daily activity may *seem* to be monotonous or even boring. It may appear that you are not doing so well in your work or your profession. It may seem that you are not appreciated in your home or that everything you do is a struggle. It may seem that your family or your associates annoy you, are unjust to you, or impose upon you. Oh, all sorts of seemingly inharmonious, imperfect, miasmic pictures may appear on your horizon, but don't be deceived. *Thine is the kingdom, the power, and the glory, and thou art exalted as head above all.*

Yes, just keep right on being aware of the Kingdom of God, which *is* your Consciousness, and you can be assured that these fallacious pictures will simply erase themselves. You don't have to erase these false appearances. You don't have to do anything about them. In fact, if you try to do something about them, they will seemingly go right on presenting themselves. What do you do then?

> You know what you are. You know that you are your own Heaven, and that this Heaven you are is your Earth, or your entire conscious Existence, right here and right now.

Don't be concerned about what the one called "another" says or does. Let your entire attention be focused upon *being* the forever living, intelligent, conscious Love that *you are*. Consider that fact that "your Consciousness is your Universe." Realize that there can be nothing in your experience that does not exist in and *as* the Consciousness that you are. Perceive that because there is no injustice, dishonesty, imposition, hatred, etc., present as the Consciousness that you are, there simply cannot be any of these fallacies evidenced in and as your experience.

Of course, you do not make affirmations and denials. Rather, it is that you are so very aware of *being* what you *are*, and *all that you are*, that you cannot be made aware of what you are not.

Oh, you will see the evidence of this wonderful revelation throughout every facet of your daily experience.

You can have full faith in this Truth. You don't prove it. You don't have to prove it. Rather, you are the living proof that this Truth is true and that *you are this Truth Itself.*

Chapter II

Home

Let us now discuss some so-called practical examples of the way in which this true Heaven that you are proves Itself to be Truth in certain specific experiences and activities. We will begin with the home.

Normally the home is considered to be the center of one's daily living. Well, it is a focal point which may be called a center; but if so, it is a center without a circumference. *You are unconfined by any circumference of any kind or nature.* Nonetheless, the predominant activity in which you are engaged may be the maintenance of the home.

Many and varied are the seeming problems that apparently confront one who is primarily engaged in maintaining a home, and this is particularly true if there are children. One of the most insidious of these seeming difficulties is the illusion that you are too confined. You may feel that your freedom is curtailed or perhaps almost non-existent. You may sometimes appear to be frustrated by the monotony and the seemingly endless little details which may appear to require your constant attention. Perhaps you may feel that you are not appreciated and that despite your best efforts and all your unselfish love, there remains misunderstanding and friction in your home. It may seem to you that there is imposition and injustice present and active in this home, or it may even seem that someone is determined to completely dominate you.

Oh, there are innumerable seeming problems that certainly appear to face the homemaker; and finally, it may appear that you succumb to self-pity, which can really seem to be devastating.

Let us now perceive the way in which this Truth fulfills Its purpose in this particular aspect of daily living. First of all, you will realize that *you are ever free.* This is true because the Universal Consciousness that you are is indivisible and limitless. There is no line of demarcation that acts as a circumference around the infinite Consciousness that you eternally are. True it is that the home may be the focal point of your fulfillment of purpose at the moment, but it is equally true that the Consciousness that you *are* exists, and exists everywhere and equally everywhere, throughout the world, this Earth, and the Universe.

You are everywhere because you are the Everywhere. No walls can contain the boundless Consciousness that you are. No environment can be a circumference. Nowhere do you begin, and nowhere do you end. Consider the fact that whatever Truth you see, or perceive, at any moment may be perceived wherever in this so-called world there is one who is ready and open for this perception. Realize that the unselfed Love that is active as your Presence is equally Love everywhere and that *you* — loving as your awareness of *being* Love—are fulfilling the purpose of Love throughout this seemingly selfish and troubled world. Oh yes, Love does fulfill Its purpose, even as Freedom also fulfills Its purpose as *you*.

What is the genuine purpose being fulfilled as a perfect home? Let us consider the many aspects of this wonderful fulfillment of purpose. In this consideration, Love must be the basic aspect. Of course, we are not speaking of a limited sense of love, which can seem to come and go and can even seem to be selfish. The Love that fulfills Its purpose in and as the Home far transcends any faulty so-called human love. It is the universal, indivisible Love that frees Its loved ones. It is this unselfed Love that is manifested as the perfect, orderly activity of the Oneness which is the Universal All, and it is in this Oneness that every star and planet moves in perfect accord, without any hint of friction or obstruction. Love fulfills Its purpose in countless ways, but one of the outstanding ways in which Love *evidences* Its fulfillment is as the home. This means your home and my home, right here and now.

This is why there is perfect harmony evidenced as everyone and every experience throughout the home. We may call it cooperation, but it is far more than that. Actually, it is Oneness, and because there is one Consciousness identified as each member of the family, this perfect harmony and peace is evident. It may appear that there are several members in a family, each one a separate individual. Well, it does

27

appear that there are innumerable stars and planets in the Universe, each one a member of the universal family, but there is one inseparable Universe. In like manner, it may appear that there are diverse members of the Body, each one a separate entity from the others. Yet there is one Body, and each member of the Body *is* the Body, even as the Body *is* each member of Itself.

Love is omnipotent. Love fulfills Its purpose in being Love by being loving, fair, just, and unselfish. There really is one living, conscious, loving Mind present as the home, and this is the indivisible Mind which is Love. The Bible says that Love is the fulfilling of the law. Indeed, this is true. Love does fulfill Itself *as* the very Principle which It is. It does fulfill Itself and evidences Its fulfillment of Its purpose in being as the living, conscious Mind of every member of your family. Therefore, we realize that the foremost fulfillment of purpose evidenced as the home is Love.

It is Love that is your inseparable Oneness. It is Love that is the living, conscious Mind of everyone in the home. It is Love fulfilling Its purpose that maintains the home in perfect peace, joy, and harmony. It is Love that frees not only you but every member of the family from any false sense of imposition, injustice, resentment, domination, or of being dominated. It is Love, *irresistible* in Its Power, that fulfills Its purpose as the perfect order and purity of the home. It is Love that fulfills Its purpose as a great abundance of *all* that is necessary to the completeness of the home.

It is Love that evidences Itself as the fulfillment of Its purpose in being, by being you and by being every one of those whom you call family. Truly, nowhere and in no aspect of our existence is the fulfillment of Love's purpose more apparent than it is right in our home. Truly, home *is* Heaven and Heaven *is* home.

God *is* Love. God *is* the Universe. God is the *only* activity and the only One that is active. This being true, Love is God. Love is the very Presence of the Power that is God and the Power of the Presence that is God.

Love is the *only* Presence, the only Power there is, as your home, and you are this Love fulfilling Its purpose as you and as everyone and as everything that comprises your home.

Love never struggles. Love never limits. Neither does Love impose or act unjustly. Love knows no resentment or hatred. Love knows nothing of selfishness or self-love. Love asks for nothing other than to *be* the Love that It constantly and eternally is. Love is Perfection and Perfection is Love. This is why our home is perfect. Perfection *is* your home.

You see, God is Perfection, and God is the very living Substance and Form of every member in your home. Therefore, there can be no imperfect substance, no imperfect form, and no imperfect activity present in the Heaven which is your home.

The following verse from the 91st Psalm has tremendous significance when understood in the light of our spiritual perception.

Because thou hast made the Lord, which is my refuge, even the most High, thy habitation; There shall no evil befall thee, neither shall any plague come nigh thy dwelling (Ps. 91:9-10).

Order is a universal, constant fact. This is an orderly Universe. Order fulfills its purpose by being orderly. There can be no disorder because such a falsity would be the direct antithesis of the order that *is*. Order fulfills its purpose in and as your home by being the very evidence of itself as an orderly home.

Beauty also is an omnipresent, universal Truth. You are this Truth. Your home is your Consciousness and the Consciousness of the integral Oneness which comprises your loved ones. The furnishings of your home may *seem* to be material things, such as furniture, objects d'art, paintings, draperies, etc. But are they material objects? Indeed, they are not. There is no matter, and that which seems to be matter is only an appearance. Yet it does signify the presence of the genuine Substance of all the Beauty that is *evidenced* in and as your home. In this way, Beauty is fulfilling Its purpose.

There is no way in which the Consciousness you are can be separated from Its manifestation or evidence of Itself. The evidence of a perfect home is Consciousness, your Consciousness and that of your family, fulfilling Its purpose by manifesting Itself *as* your perfect home.

Of course, it is possible that you may not be involved in or as a family. Perhaps your home is an apartment in which you are the only occupant, or it could be a room in a hotel. In any event, wherever you reside, whatever you call home *is* home as far as you are concerned. Thus, it fulfills its purpose as home in your experience. As stated before, your home is your Consciousness;

Now let us explore even more deeply this subject of home. Sometimes we hear someone say, "Oh, I wish I had a home." And often there does *seem* to be a great yearning for a home and what the world calls companionship. What is the spiritual significance of this seeming yearning, this apparent sense of incompleteness? Beloved, it signifies the very Presence of Love, which simply *must* fulfill Its purpose in being Love.

But make no mistake here—Love is impersonal. The sense of yearning is not what it appears to be. Rather, it is the Love you *are*, knowing that your specific purpose in being Love must be—and actually is—fulfilled. The Consciousness you are is your *only* home. Being conscious Love, your home is entirely complete. This completeness is just as entire when you are in a hotel room alone as it would be if you were in a home which included a family. You can never be separated from your home because you can never be separated from the conscious Love that you are. Knowing this, you can rest assured that everything and everyone necessary to the completeness that is your home—your Consciousness—is already present in and as the conscious Love that you are.

Home consists of all that God is. Life, Consciousness, Mind, Love, comprise the Entirety which is home. Life is the Activity; Consciousness is the Essence or Substance; Mind is the Intelligence; Love is the perfect Harmony, the inseparable Oneness.

This is your home, and this inseparable Oneness does fulfill Its purpose in being you, as well as in being your only home.

Chapter III

Business or Profession

Now let us consider another aspect of our daily affairs. Many business and professional men and women are dedicated students of the Absolute Ultimate. Sometimes it seems difficult for them to perceive just how their purpose in being can be fulfilled in their business or professional affairs.

Well, this is quite a busy Universe. In fact, every Truth that governs this busy Universe is present and active in and as every legitimate business. The impersonal Principle, which is Universal Omniaction, is present right here and now *as* the governing Principle of your business, and Love is an omnipresent Existent in and as your business.

Sometimes one will question as to just how Love can be considered as an aspect of business. If a business could exist that was devoid of Love, that business would quickly disintegrate.

You see, it is Love that is the integral Oneness of any so-called business organization. In talking with many businessmen, I have yet to find one of them who did not realize that Love was the primary basis of his business. Love and Intelligence are One, and there is no way to separate Love from Mind or Mind from Love. Certain it is that Intelligence is necessary to the successful fulfillment of the purpose of any business, but it is equally as certain that Love is necessary to this fulfillment.

It has been said that love is blind. This is a false statement. Love is not unintelligent, and neither is Intelligence unloving. Intelligent Love always acts intelligently and lovingly. Intelligent Love does not blind itself to the illusions that *seem* to present dishonesty, injustice, imposition, or the like. Never does loving Mind permit these fallacies to impose their claims in business, in the home, profession, or in any aspect of daily living. To do so would not be Intelligence in action. Neither would it be Love fulfilling Its purpose.

If we were to permit these illusions to impose upon us, we would be actually contributing to an illusory sense of existence. For instance, if some seemingly unenlightened one should attempt to impose, and if we were to permit this imposition, we would appear to be encouraging this one in his delusion. Thus, we would not be lovingly helping or alerting him to the unselfed Being that he is.

In this same way, if we were to permit dishonesty or injustice to even *appear* in or as our experience, we would be unloving. This is true because our permitting of this illusion to continue would seemingly contribute to the delusion of dishonesty. Always in situations where these fallacies seem to exist, we act firmly, intelligently, and above all, we speak and act *lovingly*. This is one way in which intelligent Love fulfills Its purpose as our business, as our profession, and as every aspect of our experience.

Good business is a wonderful fulfillment of purpose. Good business is God being busy. Therefore, this business must, of necessity, *be all that God is, in action.*

We have spoken of Love and Intelligence, or Mind. Now let us speak of Life.

Could there be a business if there were no Life? Of course not. Life is the ever-constant, undeviating activity that is ever-present and ever-active in and as every business. Sometimes it is mistakenly assumed that business is a cold, lifeless thing. There is no Truth in this assumption. Business is a vibrant, living, dynamic, moving, active aspect of the All-ness, the Oneness, that is God. Business is God fulfilling Its purpose as that specific aspect of Its Allness.

It may seem that business, or industry, is engaged in the manufacture of or the buying and selling of material things or of human services. Regardless of how it appears, there are no material "things," and there are no humans existing who can serve. Nonetheless, we know that there is something going on in the so-called business and manufacturing world. So let as discover what is going on, why it is going on, and in just what way this activity is the fulfillment of a tremendously important purpose.

Now, what is going to be written will certainly *appear* to be very human and very dualistic, but please bear with these statements for a moment, and you will perceive why it is necessary to write them in this way. Since our purpose is to realize the fulfillment of the infinite purpose in and as our daily Life and experience, we must say that which is necessary in order to reveal the indivisibility of the universal fulfillment of purpose, as our specific fulfillment of purpose right here and now. So let us continue with whatever words are necessary.

Suppose that there were no manufacturers, no industries, and no businesses. Can you imagine what it would be like to exist under such primitive so-called conditions? We would be living in caves, and a fire would have to be started by rubbing two sticks together. At nightfall we would have to be confined to the darkness of our cave because, unless there were moonlight, there would be no light. To all appearances, we would be slaves to fear, and we would be bound to our immediate surroundings. Our travel would be restricted, seemingly to the distance we could walk or run in a day.

Would there be any freedom in this way of living? Would there be freedom from fear? Would there be anything to inspire or to enlighten our existence? No. Our entire experience would be one of bondage, limitation, and fear.

Now let us bring this simile closer to home. Let us consider how it would be today if all industry and business were to cease. Suppose there were no lumber mills or manufacturers of building materials.

Suppose there were no clothing manufacturers and no company making the materials from which our clothing is made. Suppose there were no electricity, no cars, planes, railroads, or buses. Suppose there were no modern farming machinery. Suppose there were no modern home appliances.

Oh, we could go on ad infinitum with these suppositions, but our point is that business and industry are absolutely necessary right here and now as an important fulfillment of purpose. Let us now perceive the spiritual significance of the facts of this particular fulfillment.

Of course, the foregoing has to do with that which *appears* to be merely human living. But make no mistake about it, we cannot separate our daily life and affairs from the Infinite—or Universal—living, loving, conscious Mind. We partake of food, we wear clothing, we travel, and we reside in houses, hotels, apartments, and the like. We can read all night, if we wish, because there is electricity.

Oh yes, there may also be kerosene lamps or even candles, travel by wagon, and hand looms. However, our society is now geared to the more advanced areas of technology. Our necessity is to recognize these seemingly material conveniences—which make life so much easier and more free—yet to perceive that *they are not actually matter*. We must realize, though, that *they do exist as something and that they exist for the fulfillment of a glorious purpose*. We must perceive that their presence signifies many aspects of our God-fulfilling existence throughout *every* aspect of our existence. This means our universal Allness, as well as our experience, right here and now.

Everything that contributes to a more effortless existence is the fulfillment of a certain purpose. This points directly to the Truth that Life is *not* difficult. It is not necessary to struggle and strain. Jesus said, "Take my yoke upon you, and learn of me. For my yoke is easy, and my burden is light" (Matt. 11: 29-30). We know that it is right to perceive Truth and to contemplate without effort. And this same Principle of effortless Being is right, no matter what our fulfillment of purpose may be.

Does this mean that we are inactive? No! Rather, when we know — really know — what we are and what our fulfillment of purpose is, we are actually more active than we have ever been. But it is a joyous activity; it is effortless activity. It is just a steady, free, joyous busy-ness.

You can see that these "things" that seem to be material are really the means by which free and effortless activity manifests itself right here and now. You can also perceive that the telephone, radio, television, jet planes, etc., are the evidence of the spiritual fact that non-existent space is becoming less and less apparent.

But this is not all. We know that there really is neither time nor space. Travel by jet planes is a definite indication that a greater awareness of this timeless, spaceless Universe is constantly going on.

Telstar is an outstanding example of this greater awareness.

Now, all of this equipment seems to be material, but we *know* there is no matter. Yet we also know that this timeless, spaceless Universe must be revealed, and we know that this seemingly material equipment is right now bringing about a greater awareness of this Universal Truth. Thus, all of these so-called "things" are the fulfillment of a genuine spiritual purpose. Well, it takes industry and business to bring these "things" into our experience, and this is just one way in which industry and business fulfill a genuine spiritual purpose.

Anything and everything that is the means of greater freedom in and as our daily living is the fulfillment of the universal fact that freedom is an essential existent. Anything that frees us from unnecessary effort, toil, or struggle is evidence of the Universal Truth that Life is effortless. Certain it is that there is no struggle, strain, or toil in the activity of the stars and planets. Can you imagine God struggling to *be* God? Herein is the Truth that it is not necessary for you to struggle in order to be the glorious, complete, free You that you eternally and constantly are.

The homemaker, the businessman, the office worker, the laborer, the professional—all of these and many more Identities are realizing a greater sense of freedom from the bondage of incessant toil and struggle. Even though it appears that material things are the means of this realization and its evidence, the fact remains that the revelation is Spirit revealing, and the evidence of the revelation is the very Essence of Spirit—Consciousness—being.

If we contemplate and the Truth we perceive in contemplation is not manifested, our contemplation is not complete. We haven't gone far enough in our "seeing." This means that we have not realized that the Truth we perceive in contemplation is true throughout our entire existence. We have not fully realized that this Truth is evidenced in and as every iota of our daily so-called human affairs and that it is in our *everyday* living that the purpose of our revelation is fulfilled.

Let us be forever finished with a false sense of separation between our spiritual Being and Its experiences, and our Spiritual Being and Its affairs, *evidenced* right here and now. The seeming gap between revelation and manifestation *must* be transcended, and this is why this book is being written.

When we are in illumination, often we see the furniture in the room, the cars on the highway, etc. Yet we see them *as they are*. We do not see material objects. We do see Spirit, Consciousness, in form, but we also see that this Consciousness in form is active. It acts as a fulfillment of purpose. All activity is the fulfillment of a universal purpose as well as a specific purpose. All activity is intelligent, living, loving Consciousness in action. However, we cannot separate this activity from our daily experience. If we are not clear on this particular aspect of our seeing, it will *seem* that the Truth we perceive is not manifested.

Where and when should this Truth be manifested? Right here where Its manifestation is necessary to our fulfillment of purpose. When Jesus provided the loaves and the fishes in the desert, wasn't this food evident right where the need for it seemed to be? And when Jesus was said to have healed the man with the withered hand, where was the Truth that Jesus knew evidenced? Wasn't it evidenced right where that material hand seemed to be? When Jesus said, "Lazarus, come forth," where did Lazarus evidence himself? Right where he would be the fulfillment of Jesus' purpose in revealing the fact that the forever living Body is imperishable and indestructible. Jesus did not promise that Perfection would be manifested at some future time; neither did he make stipulations as to the worthiness of those who seemed to be in need. Jesus well knew that the God-Consciousness of every Identity was apparent throughout all eternity.

Chapter IV

Beauty Is Perfection

This is a beautiful Universe. Beauty is everywhere present and constantly being evidenced. Beauty evidences Itself in innumerable ways. For instance, there is the Beauty of the timeless, spaceless day or night sky; a sunset or sunrise; flowers, trees, birds on the wing, oceans, deserts, forests, etc., just to mention a few aspects of the ways in which the Universal Truth—Beauty—is evidenced.

Now, of course, all of these aspects of Beauty seem to be apparent to human sense, but the Universal Beauty that *is* always exists right where the Beauty is evidenced in our daily experience. It is because Beauty *is*, and is present right here and now, that we can see and hear the evidence of this Beauty right here and now.

Beauty can be heard as well as seen. Who has heard the song of the meadow lark, the mockingbird, the wind in the trees, the murmuring of the stream and has not heard Beauty? Well, it has to exist before it can be evidenced as the Beauty of that which is called sound. Anyone who has heard the music of the spheres *knows* the Universal Beauty that can be heard, and this Beauty is evidenced right here and now, eternally and constantly.

The artist at his canvas, the composer at his piano, the weaver at his loom, the gardener with his flowers, the woman who is gowned and groomed beautifully and tastefully—all are the fulfillment of the universal purpose of Beauty. Oh, there are so many aspects in which Beauty is evident that it is impossible to enumerate them. Wherever we see Perfection, there is Beauty, for Beauty is Perfection and vice versa. Wherever we hear genuine Beauty, we have heard Perfection, and Perfection is a universal constant. It is equally present universally because God is omnipresent and God *is* Perfection, even as Perfection is God.

Now that we are speaking of Perfection, let us pursue this wonderful subject. Certain it is that we *seem* to see, hear, and experience imperfection. This is true even pertaining to the arts. Many of the raucous noises that are called "music" today are certainly not beautiful; thus, they are not Beauty. Rather they are harsh and even ugly. This same illusory appearance applies to much that passes for modern art. Literature seems to be invaded by this apparent harshness and ugliness. In fact, the world, at the moment, seems to be in the grip of this miasma.

As we have stated, Perfection is Beauty; thus, Beauty is Perfection. Just as hatred—if it existed—would be the antithesis of Love, so it is that ugliness would have to be the opposite of Beauty. Thus, imperfection is opposed to Perfection. If we accept imperfection, we are accepting a presence that is not

God. It makes no difference whether the appearance of imperfection seems to be visible, whether we accept it as something we hear, or whether to us it appears to be something imperfect which we experience; imperfection *is not*. It does not exist because it is not God. If we give any credence to any imperfect appearance of *any* kind, we are claiming that God is not All and that All is not God. *God is Absolute Perfection and God is All.*

Of course, we can also seem to be aware of imperfect activity. For instance, some modern dances are gross and grotesque, thus ugly and a manifestation of seeming imperfection. Then too, we know certain ones who appear to be engaged in useless, purposeless, or even harmful activity. This illusion certainly is not Perfection; it is not Beauty; thus, it cannot be God. Hence, it really is not going on. There are those who seem to be actively engaged in dishonest or imperfect business practices. This is not Perfection in action, and there is no God in this kind of activity.

But what about the bodily activity? This is included in the same category. If the bodily activity seems to be imperfect, it is not God — Perfection — in action; thus, it is not genuine activity at all. Perfection *always* acts perfectly. It has to be evidenced as perfect Substance acting perfectly because of Its very Nature.

All genuine Substance — and there is no other — is absolutely perfect and beautiful because It is God,

Consciousness, Perfection, Beauty. All Substance in manifestation is the very evidence of perfect Beauty, or the Beauty of Perfection. All genuine activity— and there is no other activity—is graceful, gentle, and beautiful. It is perfect activity because It is conscious Perfection in action.

Consider the Beauty that is manifested as mountains, streams, flowers, trees, sunsets, all forms of Nature. All of this, and more than we could possibly mention, is the evidence of the perfect Beauty that *is*. Have you ever observed a field of waving grain, the graceful flight of a bird, the ripple of a stream, or boughs gently swaying in the breeze? Of course you have. Well, all of this activity is genuine. It is the Perfection that is Beauty in perfect activity. It is the Beauty of Perfection and the Perfection that is Beauty being manifested as perfect Substance in perfect activity. In short, it is the Perfection which is omniactive Omnipresence manifesting Itself as the very Consciousness that you are.

Now, of course, we know that perfect Substance is omnipresent and that perfect Substance in action —Omniaction—is everywhere and eternally present. Knowing this to be true, we can perceive that any appearance of imperfect substance or imperfect activity is an appearance only. It has no existence at all. An *appearance* is not Substance; neither is an appearance of imperfect activity Substance in action. We are often prone to accept an appearance of imperfect substance, of imperfect activity, and to feel that it must be overcome or healed. Thus, we are being deceived, even though we are very sure that we know God is All.

Whatever we accept, whatever we believe, is a matter of our own Consciousness. *Our Consciousness is our Universe.* If we imagine that we really see, hear, or experience ugliness or imperfection, it will appear that this so-called opposite of Beauty — Perfection — is our Consciousness. Shakespeare has said, "What thou seest, that thou beest," and this can certainly appear to be true. If we falsely believe that there is such a thing as ugliness, inharmony, or imperfection, we are — or seem to be — claiming this miasmic picture as our own Consciousness, thus as our own experience or body.

Let us be very alert in this matter. This alertness is exceedingly necessary now because ugliness, cruelty, and bestiality seem to be rampant. Let us not claim these illusions for ourselves by imagining that they really do exist. Of course, we do not deny that they *appear* to exist. Rather, we are so aware of the fact that All is God — Beauty, Perfection — that without even trying to know, we are aware of the fact that these false appearances have no existence.

You see, whatever you are conscious of, you are conscious of being. This is true because Consciousness is the Entirety of your Being. If you seem to be conscious of imperfection, you may also seem to be conscious of being imperfect. And if you are conscious of Perfection only, you are certainly conscious of being Perfection, which means of being perfect. Oh, beloved one, be very sure that you do not claim imperfection for—or as—your Self.

Right here an important Truth must be mentioned: you cannot claim Perfection for your Self if you even *seem* to be aware of imperfection as someone whom you consider to be another. *There is no other one.* All that you see, all that you know, all that you are aware of, *you are.*

We have often heard of practitioners who seemed to contract the very disease they have been trying to heal for "another." We have questioned why this should be. Well, the imperfection that the practitioner was trying to heal for "another" was really none other than his or her own misconception. There is much to be considered in this aspect of our "seeing."

The imperfection that appears in need of healing can seem to be the imperfect substance or activity of one called another. Yet if our attention is focused upon either the seeming imperfection or upon an assumptive "other" who is apparently manifesting imperfection or imperfect activity, this misconception is all going on within and as our own Consciousness; thus, it *appears* to be our Consciousness. This is why it can also appear to be evidenced on, in, or as *our* Body or our bodily activity.

Now we can understand why practitioners sometimes seem to manifest the diseases they try to heal.

None of these illusions are genuine, but they can appear to exist if we actually believe in them.

Chapter V

Importance of All Activity

Now let us return to our theme, *fulfillment of purpose.* It is possible for you to feel that your activity is not the fulfillment of any purpose, or at least, it may seem to you that your activity is not at all important to the fulfillment of any important purpose. Don't you be deceived. It makes no difference what your activity is, be assured that it is absolutely essential to the fulfillment of an infinite purpose and to the fulfillment of your specific purpose in being.

Suppose that you are a bookkeeper, a secretary, or engaged in any office work. Your activity is necessary to the success of the entire business, profession, or activity. Let us consider a simile. You know that any fine watch includes jewels in its works and that these jewels are necessary to the accuracy of the watch. A jewel is one of the smallest items of the watch, but it is so important to the perfect operation of the watch that it is considered an absolute necessity by all manufacturers of fine watches.

Of course, all similes are faulty, and this one is no exception. Yet it is to be hoped that it will suffice to reveal just how important *you are*, no matter what your so-called human activity may be. There is no unimportant identity. There is no unimportant activity. There is no unimportant fulfillment of purpose. Suppose there were no maids, no busboys, no janitors, no bus drivers, and no one to do the seemingly unimportant jobs that are actually so essential to the maintenance of any business. You can see how important everyone is who is employed in any capacity. I have never been more grateful for any service than for the services of maids in hotels. And I can recall at least two instances in which their loving service was of primary importance to my fulfillment of purpose in giving lectures.

Oh, sometimes it seems that we do overlook the importance of many of those who are so very necessary to the effortless fulfillment of our purpose in being. Again, let us repeat: every activity is of great importance to the fulfillment of a universal purpose and as the fulfillment of a specific purpose. So never underestimate your worth and, above all, never feel that your work is menial or unimportant.

There is another aspect of our activity that we shall now consider. The specific activity in which we are engaged today may not be exactly the same activity which may be our fulfillment of purpose next week or next year. Of course, the foregoing words are deceptive because actually there is no time, so there are no yesterdays or tomorrows. Yet it does *appear* that the nature of our business, our profession, changes as we become more aware of the limitless Identity that we genuinely are.

For instance, I was first a music student, then a music teacher, going on to become a composer and a concert pianist. Yet always there was this unsatisfied yearning for I knew not what; but during all this time my seeming search for God continued. Inevitably I came to realize what my present fulfillment of purpose was—and is. I now know that every activity in which I was ever engaged was definitely an important fulfillment of purpose, all leading to my activity in and as the Ultimate. I do not mention this in order to glorify some little inconsequential nonentity named Marie. Rather, I speak of my experience in order to bring out the parallel fact that no doubt will take place in and as your own experiences.

As our awareness of the Nature of our Being becomes ever greater, the seeming limitations disappear. We discover the fact that we are never bound or limited in any way. Students of the Ultimate are living evidence of this fact. There is nothing static or inactive in or as the experience of students of the Ultimate Absolute. In our files, there are many, many letters attesting to this fact. Why is this true?

The answer is very simple, although it involves several aspects of our study and contemplation. Of course, the basic answer to this glorious fact is that we know God is All, All is God. With this Absolute Truth as our basis, we study and we contemplate from the standpoint of the Universe. In other words,

51

we contemplate from God's standpoint rather than from the standpoint of little, limited, assumptive man. Contemplating in this limitless way, we perceive that we are immeasurable, limitless, boundless; thus, our activity—our fulfillment of purpose—is without measurements, limitations, or boundaries of any kind. Our contemplation as Universal—God—Consciousness also reveals the inseparable Nature of our Being. We perceive that our Consciousness is the one indivisible Universal—God—Consciousness and that our Consciousness in *action* is free from any divisional limitations. Later we will perceive the way in which this fact reveals and evidences itself in our everyday affairs, However, just now, let us keep our attention focused upon the universal Nature of our Being and of our purposeful activity.

Contemplating from the infinite, indivisible standpoint, our contemplation—thus, our revelation—is limitless in scope. Oh, there is power in this awareness of our universal, inseparable, Completeness, Oneness, Entirety. But be assured that this is an *active* power. Actually, it is Omnipotence in action; hence, our activity is revealed to be a power-full and limitless fulfillment of purpose. Recognizing no limitations, no divisions, we are aware only of the limitless scope of our Being.

Do you wonder how this contemplation from the universal, indivisible standpoint can be evidenced in and as your daily affairs, or how it can be evidenced as ever greater and more satisfying fulfillment of purpose? Do you wonder how this contemplation can bring forth the evidence of a more satisfying kind of employment, acceleration in your company or organization, or a change to another better, more expansive and fulfilling business or professional activity?

Well, you may be assured that all of this is possible; indeed, it is inevitable. Why? Because you contemplate from the specific standpoint as well as from the Universal standpoint. Of course, you know that this does not mean that you imagine the specific to be separate from the Universal. You do recognize the fact that the specific *is* the Universal, even as the Universal is the specific. Nonetheless, it is necessary to consider the specific as well as the Universal in all your contemplation. There are many who omit the *specific* standpoint in their contemplation, and often they seem to become discouraged because they do not experience the evidence of the Truth they perceive in contemplation. This is not surprising, as their contemplation is not complete; they have disregarded the specific in their contemplation.

Every Truth is an omnipresent, eternal, constant, Universal Truth. Every Truth is true universally, infinitely, and eternally. Every Universal Truth is also a specific Truth; every specific Truth is a Universal Truth. Thus, every Truth is true universally as well as being true specifically.

Now, you may wish to feel more assured of what is meant by the word *specific*. It is true that universal, eternal, perfect, living, conscious, loving Mind is all there is of you. Yet it is also true that this little interim in your eternal Being, which is mis-called a human life span, is but a split second in the eternity of your Being. Yet your attention *is* focused at this point during this split second.

In like manner, you know that this experience at the moment—your daily living and activity—is but a pinpoint of the universal Omniaction, which is the *you* that you are, universally active. Yet at this moment, your attention is mainly focused right here at this seeming pinpoint of your universal Being. However, there is not any division of the boundless Consciousness that you are.

Now, this that we have called a split second of your eternal Existence and a pinpoint of your uni-versal Existence is what we mean when we use the word *specific*. Please do not misunderstand our meaning here. We are not referring to a short period in "time." Neither do we refer to an area in "space." Actually, as we have so often stated, there is neither space nor time. It is indeed paradoxical that there is "here," but there is no "there." There is "now," but there is no "then." Nonetheless, we must speak in the only words that are available at the moment, so we shall speak of the "specific" as the here and the now of the focal point of your attention.

There is one important fact that must be revealed here:

The power of your contemplation is in the realization that you *are* the Universal Consciousness aware of being all that you are.

If you are clear on this important aspect of your contemplation, you will find the Universal Omnipotent Consciousness you are to be present and active in and as the specific Consciousness that you are. This is the way in which you function so wonderfully well in and as the specific Consciousness that you are, and this is why your activity is so effortless. You see, you are aware of being Universal Omnipotence Itself, actively fulfilling your universal purpose as your specific purpose at the moment.

Beloved, it will be well for you to study and contemplate much on the foregoing statements. Of course, we could have as easily stated that your Universal Identity is your specific Identity, even as your specific Identity is your Universal Identity. Yet we feel that a greater clarification has been presented in the foregoing important statements.

Now that we can further perceive how it is, and why it is, that our purpose is being fulfilled right here and now as our specific Existence, let us be what the world calls *practical*. You will recall that I mentioned the fact that our perception of being *indivisible* Universal Consciousness was revealed and evidenced in our daily affairs. Now let us see in what way this takes place.

Suppose, for instance, you are unemployed. It may even seem that there is no employment in sight.

Then, too, you may feel that your training and experience qualify you for a certain type of work or profession and that you cannot function successfully in another type of activity. Perhaps you feel that if you could just "make the right contact," you would find employment that was suitable for you.

This is a trap, beloved one, and you will not be caught in this duality, neither will you accept limitations. You *know* there is no Consciousness separate and apart from the universal, indivisible Consciousness that you are. You also know that every Identity is the very same Consciousness that you are.

You know there is no division in or as the Consciousness that you are and that you cannot contact any other consciousness, for there is no other consciousness for you to contact.

Now, what has taken place? You have perceived the glorious, omnipotent fact that anyone and everyone that is necessary to your employment—your fulfillment of purpose at the moment—is already present within and as the Consciousness that you are. You have realized that there is no "time" lapse in or as your awareness of this Truth. Furthermore, there is no "time" lapse or "space" lapse that can even seem to act as a barrier between you and anyone and everyone who is necessary to your completeness.

This same Truth is true, *and is active*, concerning your actual employment. Right now you are aware of your actual employment because right now your Consciousness is actively aware of being complete. Whatever you should know this moment, you know. Why? Because you are Consciousness. You are conscious this very moment, and the Consciousness you are right now is complete. Your completeness means the evidence of everything you should know, everything you should understand, everything that should be your employment. Yes, your completeness even means that you know whatever Truth you should know pertaining to this—or any other—situation. Oh, there is power in this knowing.

Now, when you have contemplated in the foregoing way, you may feel that you should make a phone call, write a letter, or take a walk in a certain area. Again you will realize that this is your Universal—as well as your specific—Consciousness knowing what It should know this moment. You act, without thought, according to this prompting or impulsion; and, no doubt, you will discover *why* you felt impelled to make the call, write the letter, or take the walk.

Now right here, we must be very alert. If you do any of these thing hoping you will contact someone who will be instrumental in helping you to find employment, you may be disappointed. It just doesn't work this way. You "take no thought." You simply act in this way because you feel impelled to act. It is well to give no consideration to that which seems to be the problem at this point. In your contemplation, you already have given specific attention to this particular aspect of your Existence. Let it rest right here. Don't labor it. Rather, know that your "seeing" is your "being" that which you have seen, or perceived.

Oh, wonderful things have taken place when all concern for the solution of any seeming problem is transcended. You see, once having contemplated that which is true, you know that the Truth you have perceived is evident. Therefore, you no longer are concerned about it or with it.

Suppose you feel that your purpose in your present employment is fulfilled and that now you should be active in a more expansive way. Perhaps you feel that you should change your place of employment or that perhaps you should now be active in another business or profession. Be very sure that you do not make a mistake about this normal urge to greater fulfillment. Sometimes one may wish to make a change just because he is bored or dissatisfied. There is a vast difference between being dissatisfied and feeling unsatisfied. When you feel this unsatisfied urge to be the fulfillment of a greater purpose—not for any selfish purpose but because you recognize the greater spiritual awareness you have and are—you can then rest assured that it is right. You can also be confident that you will act intelligently, unselfishly, and that it is impossible for you to make a mistake.

Just be sure that no human ambition is lurking around in your vicinity and that you know that *you of your self can do nothing*. After all, Jesus knew that of himself he could do nothing; but the glory of it is that he also knew that the God-Consciousness he was—and is—could do *all* things. Didn't he say that all power was given him in heaven and in earth? Indeed so. But he certainly was not referring to any little assumptive man.

Beloved, the All-power that is your Universal Consciousness is given—is present—right here and now as your specific Consciousness. Recognize this Truth, accept It, and you will find that It is true and It is evident right here and now in and as the fulfillment of that which *appears* to be your need— but which is actually the fulfillment of your purpose in being.

Sometimes you may wonder whether or not you should just terminate your present employment, even though nothing has as yet appeared as your expanded fulfillment of purpose. There can be no definite answer to this until it is revealed within and as your own Consciousness. Generally, though, it has been the better policy to just wait—as full open Consciousness—until the way is clearly seen *and evidenced*. However, it must also be said that it is sometimes right to just leave your present employment, knowing that already your next so-called step is revealed; but this should never be done just through dissatisfaction or boredom,

It is never right to leave any activity through a false sense of failure, inadequacy, or frustration. This illusory sense is always the little fictitious "I" seeking to assert itself, and it is this fallacious little "I" that must be completely ignored as far as any of our daily living is concerned. *You will know if it is right for you to leave whatever your employment is.* You will be so sure that you will have no choice other than to terminate your activity in that particular aspect. It is all a matter of Consciousness, your Consciousness.

Always there must be a firm faith in the Truth you know and particularly in the Self you are, knowing this Truth. It is easy to have faith in this Truth because you know that It is already true, and It is all that *is* true. But sometimes it seems more difficult to be unshakable in our faith in our Self knowing this Truth. Right here is where the recognition of the fact that *you are the whole Power of the Universal All* is of the utmost importance.

Faith in your "knowing" is faith in your Universal Being.

> Since you are aware of being the Universal All, you can have faith in the power of *being* every Truth you know.

Chapter VI

Completeness

There are other aspects of Consciousness that are exceedingly important to those who are aware that they are "seeing" *Completeness, Oneness, conscious, universal Indivisibility* beyond their present seemingly limited scope of activity. Let us consider these aspects of our Being and perceive the way in which they reveal the evidence of our fulfillment of purpose.

Completeness is one of the most important words in our vocabulary. Almost every so-called problem we seem to encounter involves the illusion that in one way or another we are incomplete. Loneliness, lack—yes, even illness and that which is called death—are all illusions of incompleteness. If it appears that you are not, at the moment, fulfilling your greatest purpose in being, it stems from this illusion. It seems that your fulfillment of purpose is incomplete. Therefore, it would be well for you to consider that aspect of your Being which is Completeness.

This is a complete Universe, and God—the Consciousness that you are—is complete as this Universe. God is Completeness; thus, *you* are complete. *Yes, you are actually Completeness Itself,* for what God is, you are. This being true, it is impossible that *any* aspect of your fulfillment of purpose could be missing from the Completeness you are. You do not have to struggle to become complete. You do not even have to try to be what you already are.

You are complete as all that you are. The only necessity is that you recognize, accept, and fully perceive the absolute fact that you are complete. Oh, if you completely perceive this glorious Truth, you will never have to seek anything. Whatever is necessary to your Completeness will be perceived to be already present, and eternally present, as the very Consciousness that you forever are.

You are complete as *what you are now.* You are complete as *all that you are now.* What you are now is the universal, conscious, living, loving Mind that you are. This is the You that you are, complete in and as the fulfillment of Its purpose in being. It is true that it appears that your awareness of being complete as all that you are is a gradual expansion of your Consciousness, but this is only a *seeming* expansion. Actually, the complete, eternal, Universal Consciousness you are is present as all that you are right here and right now. It is only because the illusion called birth has *seemed* to conceal the glorious completeness that you are that it appears you must be increasingly aware of that which you have always been, are now, and will forever be.

Knowing that right now you are complete, you can see why you need not strive to become more of what you are. You don't make an effort to become a greater fulfillment of your purpose in being. Rather, you recognize the fact that right now your purpose in being is complete. All that is necessary is that you consciously *perceive* that which you already are, and this, beloved, is what is taking place right now as you read these words of Absolute Truth. You do not need to meet anyone in order to be the fulfillment of your purpose in being. You are complete now. Everyone and everything that is necessary for this completeness is already present within and as your Consciousness. There is no other Consciousness; so the one, or ones, who are necessary at the moment are aware of—and as—the very Consciousness that you are. This realization, of course, indicates the indivisible nature of your Existence and of the Existence of everyone and everything.

You will recall that we mentioned completeness and indivisibility as two very important aspects of your fulfillment of purpose. You don't have to meet anyone; you don't have to find the right employment, the right place for your professional or business activity, the right partner, etc. *Because you are complete right now, there is nothing separating you from anything or anyone who is already your own consciousness;* but it is well to know that you are also his or her Consciousness. Therefore, that one is just as conscious of you as you are conscious of him or her. You are conscious as the one indivisible Consciousness. This is the way in which the Absolute Ultimate reveals and evidences Its Truth in your daily affairs.

The universal, indivisible You that you are always evidences Itself as just what It *is*, as the specific Identity that you are. The universal, indivisible Completeness that you are always manifests Itself as the specific indivisible Completeness that you are. If it appears that anything or anyone who is necessary to your completeness is absent or missing, be assured it is only an appearance, and it cannot even appear for very long when you continue to contemplate the indivisible Presence of the Completeness that you are.

Completeness means complete Perfection, Joy, Peace, Abundance, Vitality, Strength, and all that is necessary to Itself. But of more importance is the fact that Completeness means the Consciousness of *being* all that you *are*. Complete Consciousness is the *only* Consciousness that is conscious. Complete Life is all that is alive. Complete Intelligence is all that is intelligent. Complete Love is all that is loving. This, beloved, is the Completeness you are right here and right now.

Of course, you perceive that indivisibility is necessary to your Completeness. If it were possible for anything or anyone to be really separate from you, you could be incomplete. This is specifically true if there seemed to be a need for that one or that thing. But this is impossible, for God is the indivisible Completeness of All.

Oh, these two words, *completeness* and *indivisibility*, hold a wealth of spiritual significance. Consider them well, for they are fraught with great Light and Power.

Right now it seems necessary to recall a few salient facts. Although we have spoken of you and your fulfillment of purpose right here and now, we certainly do not wish to drop into a misconception of the Truths we have been realizing. We have not referred to assumptive human identities living in an illusory world that appears to be material. You realize that everything and everyone is really Spirit—Consciousness—being. You know that the things with which you work, the cars you drive, the furniture in your home or office, the musical instruments you play, etc., are not separated pieces of illusory matter. Matter is *not* Substance. Illusion is not substantial, neither is it active. Being nothing, it can do nothing.

You exist right here and now, and you are genuine. Everyone and everything that is necessary to your Completeness and your complete fulfillment of purpose is right here, but it consists of Consciousness—the Consciousness that you are. No matter what your activity may be, always be aware of the foregoing Truths.

Everything that is necessary to your daily activity, for your business or professional activity, or for your employment is present right here and now. Furthermore, it is present in and as Form. It is present in and as the Form that is necessary for *Its* fulfillment of purpose. Oh yes, "things" have a purpose in being, too; but things are not what they appear to be. Nonetheless, these things do exist, and they exist for a purpose.

For instance, suppose there were no pianos. What about the pianist and his fulfillment of purpose? Isn't the piano necessary? Isn't the purpose of the piano to complete the purpose of the pianist? Isn't this also true of the typewriter, the office equipment, the farm machinery, the house, the furniture, etc.? This Truth is true pertaining to innumerable things and as an infinite variety of things that are essential to our daily living,

Everything that exists has a purpose in being. There is nothing in existence that is purposeless. Nothing exists that is not necessary to some fulfillment of purpose. Every tree, every blade of grass, every flower and shrub is important. Every rock, every grain of sand, every mountain, every drop of water exists because it has a purpose to fulfill. Does this seem ridiculous? Well, let us explore this revelation, and we shall perceive that it is Absolute Truth.

The so-called lowly earthworm is of great importance to the gardener. It was once scorned, but now it is recognized to be one of the most important of all aspects of existence. (This fact is beautifully explained in a book entitled *Kinship With All Life*, written by J. Allen Boone. It is my sincere hope that you are acquainted with this book. It bears out much of the Truth we are presenting here.) But let us continue. No matter how lowly, unimportant, or even obnoxious anything may seem to be, there *is* a purpose in its being.

Once, the cactus of the desert was considered to be of little or no value. Now we have candy — delicious, too — made from the cactus. In addition to this, they are making furniture and all sorts of useful and lovely articles from these hitherto so-called useless or purposeless cacti. All of us know that sand is useful in many ways, bearing out the fact that every grain of sand exists for a purpose. Farmland and desert, mountain and valley, ocean and land — all of this, all of everything, has a purpose in being. Every day new uses are being discovered for certain minerals found in the various soils.

Oh, we could go on ad infinitum, but the foregoing will suffice to illustrate our point. It is true that we do not seem to be aware of the purpose of every aspect of Existence, but there is an ever greater awareness of this basic Truth. Of course, you know that we have not been referring to so-called dense or solid matter.

This which follows is of vital importance for all of us. *These "things" do not exist separate from or other than our own Consciousness.* All is Consciousness, and Consciousness is one integral, indivisible All. Knowing this to be true, you can see why it is impossible for you to be separate from anything that is necessary to your completeness and to the complete fulfillment of your purpose in being. Consciousness is always aware of anything It should know at any moment, and anywhere. It can be no other way because Consciousness—your Consciousness—is always aware of being the Substance of any form and the form of any Substance that is necessary to your complete, joyous, free, purposeful Existence. *This last statement is very important indeed.*

It is impossible to stress too much the necessity of perceiving the full import of what has just been revealed. For instance, in this revelation, you can see that no "time" could possibly be involved between the seeming need for anything—or anyone—and the *evidence* of whatever was necessary at the moment. The awareness that something is necessary and the evidence of the presence of that which is necessary are simultaneous. Actually, the "something" that was necessary was present in and as your Consciousness all the while, but not until it seemed to be needed was your attention called to its presence or focused upon this particular aspect of your Consciousness.

When we hear of an instantaneous so-called healing, what has really taken place? Well, conscious Perfection seemed to be the necessity at the moment. Conscious Perfection *already* existed right where and when It seemed to be absent, but it was because Perfection already existed that this Perfection could be evidenced. The attention of the so-called patient was suddenly focused upon the Perfection that did exist instead of the imperfection that did not exist.

If Jesus had been conscious of an imperfect, withered hand, that seemingly imperfect hand would have gone right on appearing to be present, but he knew *only* the Presence of the perfect hand. The Consciousness that was—and is—conscious as the one they called Jesus was not a Consciousness separate from, or other than, the Consciousness of the one who seemed to have an imperfect hand.

Jesus recognized no separate Life, Mind, or Consciousness. Rather, he perceived that the very Substance of that hand and the Substance that was his own Consciousness were *one inseparable, perfect Consciousness*. In other words, Jesus knew that this hand was his Consciousness and that his Consciousness was this hand. Knowing—being conscious of Perfection only—it was inevitable that the hand would be the very evidence of Jesus' perfect Consciousness, or of Jesus' awareness of being all Substance in Form and of being Absolute Perfection. But of course, Jesus also perceived that the Consciousness of the one who seemed to have an imperfect hand was also *his* Consciousness.

Jesus well knew the oneness of all Consciousness. He knew that the Consciousness of the one apparently standing before him was the very same—and equally the same—Christ-Consciousness that he was and is. Furthermore, Jesus knew that this one was conscious of being perfect, no matter how imperfectly aware of this fact he seemed to be.

Beloved, we cannot accept a limited consciousness as anyone or anything. There is no such thing as a limited aspect of the one all-impartial, omnipresent Consciousness,

Now, we have used the word *focus* quite frequently. Lest some misunderstanding arise about this word, let us clarify our meaning. To focus the attention does not mean to concentrate the attention. It does not mean to deliberately pinpoint our attention to any so-called little locality; neither does it mean to intentionally or deliberately meditate—or think—on any specific aspect of existence. Rather, we remain, as always, full open Consciousness. (By "full open," we mean limitless, boundless, Consciousness.)

As full open Consciousness, we find that *always* we are aware of whatever should be revealed, just when it should be revealed. Hence, if a specific aspect of Being should be more obvious in our contemplation, *we are naturally more aware of that specific aspect.*

You see, we do nothing of ourselves, even in our contemplation. We don't just decide that we are going to contemplate on one aspect of the All and deliberately confine our contemplation to this aspect. To do this would be to attempt to separate our contemplation from the one full open Consciousness and to separate the inseparable, infinite All into separate aspects of Itself. True it is that the Universal All does reveal and manifest Itself as an infinite variety of Its Allness, but it is equally true that this Entirety does not separate Itself in being complete as every aspect of Its completeness.

If God—the All—were to divide Itself into separate aspects of Itself, we would have to accept a dual God. Furthermore, we would have to believe that Omnipresence included vacuums in which there was no God. But we know that God is Omnipresence and that Omnipresence is equally present everywhere and eternally. There are no vacuums, and there can be no separateness present as the *Wholeness, the Allness, the spaceless, timeless All.*

From the foregoing, you can perceive that to focus the attention does not mean to deliberately withdraw, or "pull in," our Consciousness from the Entirety and to concentrate our attention upon one aspect of the Allness that is God. Always we remain aware of the indivisible Oneness, Totality, Entirety, in all our contemplation. But if a certain "need" or some special problem is presented, we find that our attention is focused upon the Truth that does exist in contradistinction to the "problem" which does not exist.

Now we are to investigate the subject called Supply. So let us consider this aspect of our existence as an example of what we have just been presenting.

Chapter VII

Supply

What is supply? Supply is the Presence, and the *evidence* of the Presence, of whatever seems to be necessary at the moment. Sometimes, however, it does appear that there is a necessity and neither the presence of supply nor the evidence of this presence is apparent. This, of course, presents a fallacious picture of lack, and a "lack" would be the absence of whatever was necessary. Thus, we would have the paradoxical absence of the Presence and the presence of an absence. Now, how could the Presence be absent? It couldn't. It isn't. However, we do realize that something must be clarified pertaining to supply.

We know that there can be no absence of God, who is equally present constantly and eternally. We are aware of the fact that God—our own Consciousness—is present *as* omnipresent Supply. We know that Life, Mind, Consciousness, Love are indivisibly present as our own Consciousness. We are aware that Life is Supply, Consciousness is Supply, and this is also true as Love and as Mind. Never are we unaware of this fact.

Now suppose, however, that the apparent need seems to be for the supply called money. We are already aware of the indivisible Nature of Universal Supply. Now we will find that our attention is *focused upon one specific aspect* of Supply, which is called money. We may find ourselves questioning somewhat in the following way: "What is the supply called money? Does money consist of silver, gold, copper, nickel, or paper? Is money material substance in form? Does the presence of money mean that Supply is divided? Are there really separate pieces of something called money?"

Since you know that indivisible Substance cannot be divided into pieces of substance, you perceive that money is not what it appears to be. Actually, anything that appears to be material is not what it appears to be. This is true of the Body Itself, which *seems* to consist of a separate piece of matter. *There is no matter.* So this appearance of something called money must be re-evaluated. Thus, we question: "What is here where this appearance called money seems to be?" And the answer is: "Supply."

Suppose that there is no money in sight. Suppose that it seems there is an absence of the Supply called money. If it is not visible, if it cannot be held in the hand or passed over the counter, does this mean that there is a vacuum in which there is no Supply? You know better than that. You know that Supply is as omnipresent as is God, and you also know that the very Consciousness that you are *is* Supply. So it is necessary to perceive just what constitutes Supply as the specific aspect of this Omnipresence that we call money.

When you receive a check, do you really see the money that is supposed to be in the bank to guarantee the value of the check? Of course not. The check is simply a symbol that signifies the presence of the money in the bank, but the check is not the money. You do not have to see the money that is in the bank in order to know that it exists; in fact, you do not have to be concerned with the money in the bank. Your only interest is in the Supply signified by the check. Nonetheless, the supply called the money seems to be invisible to you; you cannot feel it, touch it, or hold it in your hand.

Now, suppose that instead of a check, you hold a piece of currency in your hand. Is this piece of currency actually Supply, or is it merely a symbol that signifies the presence of something called silver or gold? When you see a five dollar bill, are you really seeing the presence of five silver dollars or of a five-dollar gold piece? No! But this leads us to the Absolute Truth as to just what money means, what it signifies.

To one who seemed to be in dire need, that five-dollar bill would appear to represent a lot of money. To one who seemed well-supplied, it would look very small indeed. Yet the value of the five-dollar bill would not have changed at all. Our point is that this piece of currency represented supply according to each one's concept of supply.

Let us take another look at this piece of currency. Let us consider it in terms of supply. To one it would appear to be a lot of supply. To one (called another) it would appear to be a little supply. Its value would depend upon the concept of the one who held it in his hand.

Now, in either case, was that five-dollar bill actually Supply, or did it merely signify the presence of Supply? Was its value ever more or less, or was its value entirely within and as the Consciousness of the one who beheld it? If that five-dollar bill were really Supply, why would it purchase much in goods and services in one country and very little in another country? Oh, we can realize many ways in which it is evident that the appearance called money is not really Supply.

Now, of course, you realize that the foregoing sounds very materialistic, thus very dual. But bear with us for a moment, and you will see why we had to use these similes.

Money is not Supply; but even the appearance of something called money signifies the Presence of Supply. What is Supply? Supply is a Universal Principle. It is a Universal Constant. It exists everywhere and eternally. It is present equally everywhere. It does not fluctuate. It is never more nor less. It can never be absent, for it is Omni-presence.

When we appear to "see" a piece of money, silver, gold, currency, etc., we are looking right at the whole Principle that *is* Supply. To us, it may appear to be limited to one dollar or five thousand dollars, yet the actual Presence of Supply, right where that so-called money appears to be, is limitless. It is not limited in value. It is not divided into bits of Itself. It is *all the infinite Supply in existence*, regardless of what figures may appear on something that looks like a piece or pieces of currency. Never can It be any more or any less. Never can It be absent. Always It is *complete as All that It is*. Never can It be depleted or exhausted.

Again and again, we have said, "God is my supply." In this very statement, we have seemingly separated our supply from our own Being. Why? Because it is a dualistic statement. It implies that God is something separate from or other than your own Being, and it also implies that God can supply you with something that you need. This simply is not true. God is the Entirety of your Being, but you are also the Being that is God.

What is your Supply? *You are.* The Consciousness that you are is the Supply that you are. The Supply you are can no more be absent than you can be absent from your Self. Consciousness *is* Substance. You are conscious. The Consciousness you are *is* the Substance of the Supply of anything that is necessary to your Completeness and to your complete fulfillment of purpose. *This is Absolute Truth.* Now let us perceive how it is that this Absolute Truth evidences Itself in and as your everyday experience.

You realize that you exist as the fulfillment of a universal, as well as a specific, purpose. Right now, and right here, you *are* the fulfillment of your purpose in being.

Something that the world of appearance calls money is certainly necessary to your fulfillment of purpose. You are not deceived. You know that you cannot possess Supply; thus, you know that you cannot possess money. Yet Supply signified by the appearance called money must be abundantly perceived and evidenced. It would not be possible for you to exist as a joyous, free, normal Identity if you were limited in *any* way. If the appearance that signified the Presence of Supply were limited, your fulfillment of purpose would be limited. Thus, there can be no limitation of that which is called money.

You may wonder why it is that limitation seems to be your lot. You may also wonder why John Jones, who is so undeserving, has so much money and you have so little. (Oh, I know this sounds dual, but we must clarify this matter.)

No doubt John Jones seems to be limited in many ways unknown to you. Perhaps his health seems to be limited, or he may seem to be limited in joy, peace, or a harmonious home situation. But if he seems to be well-supplied with money, it simply means that this aspect of his existence is not so limited. He may be more aware of being Supply in the form and substance called money than he is of other aspects of Supply.

It does seem — until we know better — that every one of us is limited in one or another aspect of daily living. It also seems that each one of us is less limited in one aspect of supply than in others. Limitation of the awareness of, and the evidence of, that aspect of supply called money is but one small facet of this illusion that we are separated, bound identities.

In the first volume of this work, we have spoken of Supply as being Life, Health, Joy, Peace, etc., so we will not repeat that which has already been said. But we will continue with our exploration of Supply that is symbolized by the appearance called money.

Now we are going to get right to the very basic Principle of what does exist right here and now as that which appears to be material substance in the form of money. Don't be startled. We are not going to pretend that matter is Spirit or vice versa. We know there is no matter, but we also know there is something here that the world of appearance calls money. Let us see what it is.

When we are illumined, we see things as they are and not as they appear to be. For instance, a rock that appears to be solid, dense matter when we are not consciously illumined, is known to be otherwise when seen as it actually is. Illumined Consciousness reveals that it is not solid; it is not dense or heavy. Certainly it is not dark; rather, it is Light. But it does have outline, and we know what it is. We know it is that which the world calls a rock. It is in this same way that we see the body of a tree or the Body of anyone or anything.

Now, a so-called piece of money exists in form, so it is a body. Have you ever looked at a dollar bill when you were illumined? If so, you know that it is not what it appears to be to those who seem to be seeing materially. You see the form, or the outline, but you do not see anything solid or dense as its Substance. Rather, you see that it is Light in form. But this is not all. As with everything that you see as illumined Consciousness, you see that it is intensely active. You couldn't describe this activity. Yet you actually *see* it, and you know it is going on. But most important of all is the fact that *you know you are the very substance of that which is called a piece of currency, and you are not matter.*

You are not seeing matter; neither are you being matter. You are seeing what you are being, and this is Consciousness. You are being what you are seeing, and this is Consciousness. You are aware of the fact that the very Consciousness that you are is the Substance in Form that comprises that which appears to be a dollar bill. You are aware of being limitless Substance. You are aware of being absolutely free, boundless, and without limitations of any kind.

It is in this glorious, illumined experience that you really perceive the limitless nature of Supply in the aspect called money, and it is in this same illumined "seeing" that you perceive the absolute fact that Supply is ever-present, indivisible, and oh, so abundant.

In this awareness, you realize that whenever you look at any so-called aspect of money, you are really seeing the whole principle that is Supply. You know it cannot be possessed because It is indivisible. If anyone were to offer you all the money in the world, you would merely smile. You know that you—the Consciousness you are—are the very Principle which is all the Supply in Existence. You know that the Supply you are is as limitless, as boundless, as is the Consciousness you are, and you know that no one could possess this Supply any more than anyone can possess the air or the sunlight. All of this you know, and you *know* that you know. But there is much more that you cannot put into words.

Beloved, I have hesitated to say the things I have just said. I well know that this may be misunderstood and that there may be some who will falsely imagine that I am trying to make matter into Spirit or vice versa. Nonetheless, I have had no choice. These Truths had to be stated, and I know you will realize that I understand the portent of the foregoing paragraphs.

You see, the illusion of financial limitation has seemed so real to so many dedicated students of Truth, and it has seemed to be one of the most difficult aspects of illusion to disperse. I have long known that it would someday be necessary to make these statements. All of us have the right—even the necessity—to be free from the false anxieties of limited supply.

When we see a piece of currency as illumined Consciousness, we know that it does not represent just a limited supply of money. We know that the Supply it represents is not limited to that which is called one dollar, five dollars, etc. Rather, we know that the piece of currency represents—and is—the whole principle of Supply.

Now I have finished with this subject. It is my sincere hope that you will study and contemplate frequently and deeply the Truths that you have just read. You see, the Truth that has just been revealed is the complete answer to a false sense of lack or limitation of *any* kind.

And there is another fact that I can tell you: if you can accept fully and without reservations the Absolute Truth revealed in the foregoing statements, never will you be deceived again by any fallacious claims of lack or limitations. Whenever you look at a dollar bill, you will not limit the Supply you perceive to one dollar or even to one thousand dollars. Rather, you will know that you are actually seeing and being all the infinite Supply in Existence. All of this you will know because you will be aware that the Consciousness that you are is the Substance, the Form, and the Activity of all Supply.

We have said that everything—all Substance— exists for the fulfillment of an infinite, as well as a specific, purpose. We have perceived that all Substance exists in and as Form. No Substance comes into being, and no Substance goes out of being. We know that Consciousness is the *only* Substance. No matter what the Form may be, the Substance of the Form is Consciousness. Consciousness in Form is the Substance of everything we see or experience. All Substance in Form exists for the fulfillment of a specific, as well as for the fulfillment of an infinite, purpose. Houses, trees, cars, planes, bridges—more aspects of Existence than we could possibly mention—all of these exist as Form for the fulfillment of purpose. What is the universal purpose that is fulfilled by this eternal, perfect Substance manifested as Form? *Supply.* Supply is an eternal Existent. It is an eternal Constant, without interruption.

If the Universe lacked one iota of Its omnipresent, eternal Supply, It could not completely fulfill Its purpose in being. If you lacked one iota of the omnipresent, eternal Supply that you *are*, you could not completely fulfill your purpose in being.

Universal Consciousness is the Substance of Itself. Thus, It is the Substance that is Its own constant, uninterrupted, eternal Supply. The Consciousness you are is the Substance of all the Supply necessary to your constant fulfillment of your purpose in being.

Do you wonder why Supply is necessary to the fulfillment of purpose of the Universal All? Well, this Universe has to be Self-maintaining, Self-sustaining, in order to be perfect and eternal. There is nothing outside of, or other than, this Universal All.

Therefore, the very Substance that *is* this Universal Entirety is Its own Supply. The Supply that Universal Consciousness *is*, is necessary to Its eternal, uninterrupted purpose in being. This is evident in the fact that the Universe is ever fresh and new. Indeed, It is Its own Newness. This is why you are ever fresh and new. The Consciousness that you are is the Supply that you are, and it is this ever new Consciousness that you are that fulfills Its purpose as you by being constant, eternal, omnipresent Supply.

Supply does exist in and as Form, and It does exist in and as any and every Form that is necessary at any given moment. This is Absolute Truth. If the seeming need is for a car, the Supply—Consciousness in Form—that you are, is present *as* the car. If an apartment or a house seems necessary to your fulfillment of purpose, that apartment or that house is the Supply that is your own Consciousness in Form right here and right now.

Let us, as briefly as possible, present a very simple simile of the fact we have just stated. One night when I was to give a lecture, I was just leaving my room in the hotel to go to the lecture hall. Suddenly, something happened that necessitated the presence of a pin. Apparently there was no pin in the room, and I could not wait to call for the services of a maid, as I was due in the lecture hall at once. I found myself saying, "Well, a pin is the necessity right now, so a pin just has to exist as my Consciousness right now."

Suddenly, I saw something shine on the floor just at the edge of the baseboard, and I walked over and picked up a pin. Now, where was that pin? It was in and as the Consciousness that I am. Why didn't I see it before? Hadn't it been right there all along? The necessity for the pin had not appeared before. When this necessity appeared, I was aware of the pin because my attention was focused upon that which seemed to be necessary. I was not really aware of the *absence* of the pin; rather, I was aware of the fact that the pin already existed as the Consciousness that I am. If there had been no necessity for a pin, I would probably have departed from the hotel without ever noticing this Supply—as a pin—which was right there before I ever seemed to need it.

"Before they call, I will answer; and while they are yet speaking, I will hear" (Isa. 65:24). Who is it that answers even before the call? The God-Consciousness you are is the Consciousness that recognizes the presence—in any form—of anything that is necessary to your complete fulfillment of purpose.

Whenever a need appears for any specific "thing," your attention is focused on that thing. Your Consciousness is your Universe, and your Consciousness is ever complete. Now, when your attention is focused upon anything, it means that the very thing is already present in or as your Consciousness. If it had not been already present, you would not have been aware that it was necessary. Thus, the thing that is necessary existed in and as the Consciousness you are, before you seemed to need it. It was only the "seeming" need that drew your attention to the fact that it already existed.

From the foregoing, you can perceive that there is never a "need." Rather, there is *always* the Supply, and instantly your attention is focused upon anything that is necessary, you discover that the Supply is right here and now within and as your Consciousness. Furthermore, It exists in and as any Form that is necessary to the fulfillment of Its purpose.

There is an outstanding example of this Truth recorded in the life of Jesus. You will recall that he was preparing to go into the city to partake of the Passover with the disciples. (The Passover seems to be a very human event, but there is a tremendous spiritual significance beyond this seemingly human event.) However, Jesus sent the disciples into the city to make preparations for the Passover. He told them they would see a man bearing a pitcher of water and that they were to follow him:

> And he will show you a large upper room furnished and prepared: There make ready for us" (Mark 14:15).

Where was the man bearing the pitcher of water? Where was the upper room? They existed within and as the Consciousness of the one called Jesus. It seemed there was a need for this upper room; thus, Jesus' attention was focused upon the room.

If the room had not already existed, Jesus would not have been conscious of it. The man with the pitcher of water and the upper room were already present in and as the Consciousness of Jesus. Thus it is with us. Now, let us state this glorious fact in some absolute statements that you can contemplate frequently.

> Whatever you are conscious of, you are conscious as that thing. You are conscious of being that which claims your attention at any moment.

If a seeming need claims your attention, it can only mean that you are conscious of that which is the Supply for that specific necessity. Since you are conscious *of* the Supply, you are conscious *as* this Supply. This is true because the Supply already exists as the Substance that is your own Consciousness. Yes, it exists as the Substance in Form of what is necessary. It has always existed as your Consciousness because it *is* your Consciousness. When there is a necessity for It to appear as Substance in Form, your attention is focused upon that particular aspect of your Substance — which is your Consciousness.

Never put the seeming need before the Supply. Always acknowledge the presence of the Supply in whatever Form is necessary. That which seems to be a need simply serves to draw your attention to the Supply which is already here. In other words:

Your Consciousness is your Universe; your
Universe is your Consciousness.

It is true that these "things" appear to be matter
in form. Yet even the physicists know that there is
no matter as such. Thus, there is no matter existing
in or as *any* form. There *is* Substance in Form, but
this Substance really is Consciousness, and this Substance in Form is Consciousness in and as a specific
Form. Always realize, though, that Consciousness is
indivisible and that Its Presence as Form does not
mean that It exists as separate forms of Itself.

Now, you will note that I have frequently used
the expressions *your Consciousness* or *my Consciousness*.
I have even referred to *Jesus' Consciousness*, but this
does not mean that Consciousness is, or can be,
possessed by anyone. You do not possess Consciousness. Yet you are conscious. This is true because you
are Consciousness. So whenever you read the words
your Consciousness or *my Consciousness*, you will
realize that this terminology is not used in any
possessive sense. It is used only for the sake of
brevity.

In this same way, you will recognize the fact
that you do not possess Life, Mind, or Love. Yet you
are alive, intelligent, and loving because you *are*
Life, Mind, Love. This has been stated before, but it
is well to frequently remind oneself of this Truth.
You see, the very moment it seems to us that we
possess anything, we have seemingly dropped into

dualism. We have imagined that Existence is separated into loves, consciousnesses, minds, and lives. It also appears that Substance is divided into separate "things" which we can either possess or lack.

Chapter VIII

Consciousness Is Inseparable

What is it that makes everything appear to be separated or divided? It is the way we *seem* to see, hear, touch, smell, and taste. Yes, it can even be in the way we seem to experience things. A so-called separate body can seem to experience a separate pain that belongs to it alone, or a so-called separate human being can seem to experience his separate sorrow, trouble, or his seeming problem of any nature.

Often we hear of the five physical senses. Actually, if there were *any* physical senses, we would have to accept the fallacy of many aspects of these non-existent senses. We have frequently stated that there is one Sense and this Sense is Consciousness. There are innumerable aspects of this one Sense, Consciousness, but every aspect *of* Consciousness *is* Consciousness.

Who is it that appears to see, hear, touch, taste, or smell these things that seem to be matter? What mind knows anything about them? If anyone were really aware of these so-called physical senses, God, the infinite All, would have to be aware of them. If God could be aware of such illusions as materiality presents, God would have to be the illusion and the mind that was deluded.

If man is aware of birth, sickness, age, deterioration, or death, then God must be aware of being a temporal God, forever beginning, changing, becoming imperfect, aging, and dying, only to have to begin all over again. The infinite Mind that is God simply does not know anything at all of these illusions. Since the All-Consciousness knows them not, we do not really know them either. How can we know anything that God does not know?

Now, let us see who—or what—it is that seems to have these so-called physical senses. *It is merely a supposititious consciousness or mind that presents itself as a fraudulent substitution for a genuine Mind.* It is comprised of sheer illusion rather than being the forever perfect, conscious Mind which we are. It is as though a universal mist or mirage were superimposed over our whole Universe, which makes it appear to be different from or other than the eternal, perfect, immutable Universe which does exist.

Who is it that seems to be the victim of this universal fraud? The assumptive born man, who is nothing but a simulation of the eternal, conscious, living Mind which really is Man. The only Man there actually is, is the Christ-Man. A born man is not a Substance, is not Intelligence, is not Consciousness, Life, or Love. Thus, there is no conscious, living, intelligent, loving, born man. A supposedly born man, consisting of illusion, can only see, hear, touch, taste, smell, or experience his own illusions. But this supposedly born man is not *you*. It is not the *I* that you are. It is not the *I* that I am. Thus, it is actually nothing. Nonetheless, because it seems so real, we must clarify even its pretenses.

Beloved, please know that it is not easy to say what now has to be said. I know full well how unrealistic—even ridiculous—many of the following statements are going to seem. I also know that some statements will sound exceedingly dualistic. But you will realize that when I am speaking of "man with breath in his nostrils," I must sound dualistic because this pseudo kind of man is the very basis of all duality.

Nonetheless, you will know that *no such man exists*; thus, the whole exposal and disposal of this simulated man is really but the prelude to the glorious, full perception of the eternal, perfect, immutable Christ-Man that you genuinely are. This Christ-Man knows nothing of duality or any of its fraudulent pretensions. Always though, you will know that there are not two of you, one that is simulated and another that is genuine. You are forever One, and there is no second you.

Now let us say what must be said: *birth is a complete fraud.* There is no birth, no born man, and no one who knows himself to be, or to have been, born. There is no mind that knows anything of birth. There is no one who knows anything of a born body. A born body is but a simulated appearance that stems from the universal, miasmic mirage which is neither substance, life, nor activity.

Creation is a word that could very well be omitted from our vocabulary. There is *no creation* because there is *no creator*. God is not a creator; thus, man can never be a creator. Since All eternally *is*, what purpose would be served by a creator or a creation? None! Any seeming birth stems from the universal illusion that there is a creator, thus, a creation. If we are ever going to be completely free from the so-called last enemy, the final illusion, we must be aware of the fact that the word *creation* implies something that simply is false and completely fraudulent.

Inherently we know that death is not necessary. No one really wants to accept death. Yet it seems that most of us insist upon believing the falsehood of birth. We can't have one without the other. If man is or could be created or born, man would of necessity have to die. Anything that begins must also have an ending. But a created—or born—Man is just as fraudulent as is a God who is said to be a creator.

It is this supposedly created, or born, man who seems to see, hear, and experience as though he were a separate identity. It is also this simulated man who appears to see and to experience separation and division of everything and everyone. To him everything in form appears to be blocked off into large or small blocks of solidity, or matter. This same deceived and deceptive born man imagines that he is limited, bound, and measurable in terms of time and space. He is fearful, doubtful, perturbed, and disturbed by all the delusions of trouble, sickness, lack, age, etc., that inevitably accompany the illusion of having been created or born. But perhaps the most hopeless aspect of all his illusion is that he is sure that he must die. Why? Because he is certain that he was born. *There is, there can be, no God in anything so hopeless and so tragically deceiving as this assumptive born man.* So this kind of man is entirely a myth. But let us see further into the illusion in order that we may be through with it forever.

All that seems to be apparent in and as this illusory, simulated world of materiality is temporal. Being temporal, it is necessarily limited in all ways. It is not conscious Mind, so it can have no awareness of what it is, nor can it really know anything. Being completely an *assumptive* man, all it can do is to assume. It can seem to assume that it knows something, that it is alive, that it is conscious, that it loves, or is in love. It can also apparently assume that it is sick, aged, unhappy and that it must die. It can assume that there are opposites such as good and bad, joy and sadness, peace and turmoil, love and hate, etc. It can assume that there is God *and* man.

Let us now know what is the Truth concerning all of this. *There are no opposites; therefore, there is no opposition.* There are no separate born beings to be opposite or to oppose each other. There is no such thing as God *and* man. There is no "otherness." There is only the one undivided, eternal One, *and You are that One.*

Before birth, you knew what you were. You knew that you were eternal, perfect, indivisible, and one inseparable Entirety. Then it seemed that you were born, and thus it appeared that you became two instead of one. As the fraudulent world of appearance continued to submerge or envelop you, you seemed to forget the eternal *I* that you knew yourself to be before birth. In fact, you appeared to become more and more aware of the things of the universal, simulated mirage than of the genuine and only universal Allness that really *is* and is the entirety of your Being and Body.

When we seem to be immersed in this false covering, we do not see things as they really are. Those seeming pieces of matter called born bodies are no more genuine, and they are no more alive, than are the puppets on the end of the strings operated by a puppeteer. They can seem to be made to do all sorts of silly things.

These puppets can be likened to animated cartoons. They can appear as ridiculous or distorted shapes or substances. They can appear to act intelligently or unintelligently. They can appear to be either good or evil. Yet they are completely devoid of Life, Intelligence, or Love. Thus, of themselves they are nothing.

The illusion called birth seems to make us aware of a non-intelligent, imperfect world. It also presents all sorts of phantasmic pictures, some of them good and even attractive. Others appear to be very bad indeed. No matter how these fallacious pictures appear to be—either good or bad—they are simply pictures that appear and then must disappear.

Furthermore, they are not pictures of you, of me, or of anyone or anything. You simply are not the substance, form, or the activity that is depicted by these fictitious pictures. What are these pictures? They are merely the altogether fraudulent, simulated, universal miasma making animated cartoons from its own mirage. Where are you? *Right where the altogether false picture of you seems to be.* (Actually, of course, You are everywhere, but the Body you are is a focal point of the infinite You that you are.) Nonetheless, these animated cartoon figures are *not* the eternal, perfect Body that you are.

As previously stated, before the miasma of birth, we were One. We knew what we were as this indivisible, Universal One. Then it seemed that we forgot what we were and knew our Self to be. Thus, our necessity is to remember what we were—and knew our Self to be—before that illusion which is called birth.

Make no mistake about this word *memory*. Memory has nothing at all to do with a human mind. It is generally believed that memory is located in a so-called human brain and that it normally remembers past human events, scenes, or experiences. Consciousness does not remember. It is conscious. It is aware. Consciousness is Mind, even as Mind is Consciousness. Instead of a so-called born human mind with its illusory memories, there is the infinite, omnipresent, Conscious Mind that is all knowledge. Thus, this Mind—which you are—is conscious of anything It should know at any moment. It is never a matter of human memory; rather, it is always a matter of being conscious of that which you already, and forever, know.

But we must not diverge from our primary subject just now. Suffice it to say that to remember means to be conscious right now of that which does exist, that which is going on now and eternally. In this sense only can we use the word *memory*. You see, it only *seems* that we forget the heaven we knew before the world of illusion—birth—seemed to begin for us. It only appears that we become unconscious of the way we *are*, the way everything and everyone eternally *is*. In illumination, we are aware of the fact that the kingdom of Perfection is all that is ever here. Thus, as illumined Consciousness, we remember the Truth that we seem, for a brief moment, to have forgotten.

In *The Gospel According to Thomas*, Jesus states the foregoing very clearly. On page twenty-six of this priceless book, we read, "… the dead are not alive and the living shall not die." Wonderful words of Truth are these. These little, distorted, animated cartoon figures are not alive because they do not consist of living, loving, conscious Mind. This is only an *appearance* of death. But, Beloved, this appearance is the only death there is or can ever be. We are right here consciously alive, right now in the midst of these fallacious, false images; and the fact that we are alive is proof that there is no death. Of course, the eternal, conscious, living Mind that we *are* right here and now cannot die.

Jesus continues, "In the days when you devoured the dead, you made it alive." Yes, it was only our seeming recognition and acceptance of this world of *appearance* that made it even *seem* to be alive, to be intelligent, or conscious. We do seem to keep it alive by clinging to the illusion that it is real. In this way, we appear to feed it, thus to maintain and sustain it.

An illusion has to have someone to be deluded by it in order to even be an illusion. When we are fully enlightened, we no longer even seem to be deluded. Thus, the illusion has nothing to feed it, to sustain it, or to maintain it. Inevitably, then, it is obliterated. It no longer even seems to exist. On the next to the last line of this page, Jesus questions:

> On the day when you were one, you became two. But when you have become two, what will you do?

Yes, what will we do? Beloved, we will do exactly what we are doing right here and right now. We will continue in our realization of the fact that eternally we *are* One and not two. Thus, this seeming phase of dualism is obliterated.

Beloved, right now we are "remembering" what we were, and knew our Self to be, before the miasmic world of illusion seemed to engulf us. In every word of Truth we read, hear, or utter, we perceive the genuine and only Universe—the indivisible Oneness of all Existence. In every contemplation, we are conscious of being the eternal, changeless, Self we have always known and know our Self to be.

An illusory misconception has not changed the Identity we are into a born, mortal identity or body. The simulated, universal mirage has not made us unconscious. We are the very same Consciousness we were before the illusory mirage ever appeared. We will continue to be this same perfect, eternal Consciousness when the completely false mirage is obliterated. We are not deceived by any illusory cartoon pictures. We see right through these fallacies, and we really see things as they are. We do not see with so-called human vision, nor do we hear with the ear of man. We see, we hear, because we are the Consciousness that *perceives*, and what we perceive as this infinite, inseparable Consciousness is that which is ever perfect, glorious, and eternal.

We know that the Existence we see, hear, experience, and know is not visible to the assumptive vision of man. Yet we know that this perfect Existence is visible. It can be seen and It *is* seen, clearly and distinctly. As enlightened Consciousness, we see this perfect, eternal Universe, this—and every—perfect Body *as It is*; and never can we be deceived by any superimposed simulation of this forever beauteous, glorious, perfect Body. We *know*, and we know that we know. We know that we *are* what we know, and we know nothing else. There is naught else to know.

Oh, there is great power in what we are realizing right now. What we are seeing — perceiving — this very moment means the dissolution of the seeming mist. What is the mist? It is the universal, or mass, mirage which makes things *seem* to be other than they are. It is merely a mistaken concept, or misconception, of what Man genuinely and eternally is.

In our Bible we read:

> But there went up a mist from the earth, and watered the whole face of the ground. And the Lord God formed man of the dust of the ground, and breathed into his nostrils the breath of life; and man became a living soul (Gen. 2:6-7).

These two verses from Genesis tell the whole story. Man, the Christ, already and eternally existed, and *is*, right now. The Universe — the glorious, perfect, eternal, Universe — was and *is* complete. Yet there does seem to be a simulated, fraudulent mirage which conceals this glorious Universe and the Substance in Form of everyone and everything. This mass illusion is clearly described in these verses. And here also we have the record that illusory man, with breath in his nostrils, was formed from the very dust of the ground, which had absorbed the phantasmic mist. Here, God is depicted as being a creator. In this very misrepresentation, Life is supposed to enter the body of man; Soul is supposed to have entered this body. The illusion that man is a creator or a creation is based squarely in this illusory picture presented in Genesis.

Soul is Consciousness. Soul is alive. It is a living Substance because Consciousness is Substance and Consciousness is Life. Soul, Life, can never *enter* the Body, for living Consciousness is the eternal, perfect Substance which *is* the Body.

Chapter IX

Body

Where is this Body that consists of living, conscious Mind? Right here, where a created body seems to be. It is true that It does not appear to be visible. Why? Because the fraudulent mirage seems to conceal It.

It appears that a mist—mistaken sense of body—covers It, hiding It from view. But never mind. *This Body can be seen and is seen by the eye that is single.* It is seen by the undivided, inseparable Vision that is Spirit, Consciousness. But you may ask, "How do we know that this Body actually exists, if we do not actually see It? Suppose we are not illumined? Suppose we do not yet see with the single Eye. Have we any way of knowing that the eternal, perfect Body does exist right here and now as this Body?"

Indeed, there is a way in which we can be assured that this eternal, perfect Body does exist, and this way of "knowing" is literally fraught with power. Let us perceive the way in which this Body can be apparent in all Its glory.

Beloved, let us seem to descend for a moment in order that we may ascend to ever greater heights of spiritual perception. We know that there *is* something right here where this appearance of solidity called the body is so apparent. We know that this, right here, is no vacuum. We know there is Life here because, obviously, there is activity. Life *is* activity, and without Life, there could be no activity. Thus, there can be no doubt but that there is Life right here where this false covering seems to be.

Now Life, in order to fulfill Its purpose in being Life, has to be alive, and It has to be alive as the Life of a living Substance. We know that we are conscious and that we are conscious of being right here where Life is alive. Thus, we are conscious of being right here where a mirage — or mistaken sense of body — appears to be. This being true, the Consciousness we are does exist here and now, right where the Life we are is evident as activity. Consciousness is inseparable from Life. Consciousness is Substance. The living Substance which is alive right here and now *is* this glorious Body that seems to be concealed at the moment.

We know that neither Life nor Consciousness can ever have entered, or have been born into, this Body because It consists of living Consciousness. Another name for Consciousness is Soul. Soul being the Substance of this Body, It could not possibly enter the Substance that It *is*, nor could It depart from the Substance that It is.

We know that Life, Consciousness, Mind, Intelligence, Love, are one inseparable, integral Entirety. So we know that this Body is comprised of Mind, or Intelligence, and Love as well as consisting of living Consciousness. The Body of the Universe, without a circumference, consists of Life, Mind, Consciousness,

Love. This Body right here consists of Life, Mind, Consciousness, Love. The universal Body *is* the specific Body, and the specific Body is the universal Body.

As we know, we are alive, conscious, intelligent, and loving, right here *as* the very Substance in Form that is this Body and Its *only* activity. Can Life be seen by so-called human vision? Can the eye of "man with breath in his nostrils" see Mind, Intelligence, or Love? Is Consciousness visible to eyes that seem to see only matter? Indeed, no. It follows, then, that the Substance of this Body which is comprised of living, loving, intelligent Consciousness is invisible to the human sense of vision. Yet we know that living, loving, conscious Mind does exist right here because we are aware of being alive, conscious, intelligent, and loving.

> From the foregoing, we can perceive that the seemingly invisible Substance in Form is the Body, while the seemingly visible substance in form is not the Body.

It is simply a miasmic appearance that seems to conceal the Body that *is*. It is this fallacious misconception of body that seems to blind us to the Body that is actually present. Once this entirely false sense of body is transcended, the Body that has seemed to be invisible is clearly visible.

Why is this true? It is true because the Vision that sees this eternal Body is the very same Essence that comprises this Body. It is Spirit, or Consciousness, perceiving Itself as Its own Substance in Form. This is what it means to see when the "eye is single." And, as stated in the Bible, it is this spiritual Vision that reveals the whole Body to be "full of Light." Of course, it is full of Light because it *consists* of Light. This Light is your enlightened, or illumined, Consciousness. This Body of Light is comprised of the living, intelligent, loving Consciousness that you genuinely are.

As we have said, the Substance of this Body is invisible to assumptive man, who seems to see materially. But this apparently invisible Substance is Power.

> It is Power because It is the Presence of Omnipotence. It is the only Power because It is the only Presence. Only that which is present can be Power.

It is never that which seems to be visible that is power. Rather, it is always the Presence of that which seems to be invisible that is Power. But this seemingly invisible Presence is also indivisible. It is not confined within the outline that delineates the Body. Neither is there anything existing as this delineation that excludes the Universal Presence from the Body. We can say that It is indwelling, but we must also perceive that it is the *All-dwelling* Presence.

The indwelling, all-dwelling, invisible, indivisible Presence is the Power that remains forever perfect as this Body right here. It is this invisible Presence that eternally maintains and sustains this perfect, changeless Substance in Form, constantly and eternally. It is this invisible, omnipotent Presence that is ever intelligently active, governing the Substance It is, in perfect order and harmony.

That which is called matter is never alive. It is nothing but a fraudulent appearance, and an appearance can never be alive. It can appear to be either perfect or imperfect, young or old, sick or well. Yet it is none of these things. Being only an appearance, it can only *appear* to be. Nonetheless, an appearance cannot forever even *seem* to conceal the perfect, eternal Body that does exist.

Do not be deceived. Have no doubt whatever but that this seemingly invisible, indwelling, all-dwelling Presence is genuine. It is a tangible, living Essence, and It exists in and as Form. It is alive. It is the *only* Substance, right here and right now. It consists of living, perfect, conscious Mind. It is ever new, yet ever the same Essence. Perfect conscious Mind is a genuine, living Essence, and It is alive forever. This Essence in Form is your eternally perfect, immutable Body. Furthermore, It is eternally alive, active as your *only* Body.

Let our faith be in that which is seemingly invisible rather than in that which is seen by the so-called human eye. This is exactly what Paul meant when he said, "Now, faith is the substance of things hoped for, the evidence of things not seen" (Heb. 11:1).

Indeed, the living, conscious Mind that is imbued with and as this faith is the very Substance of this Body of Light. And we can be assured that this Substance really is evident, when It is seen by the Consciousness that is illumined. But even if we have not yet consciously seen this eternal, changeless, perfect, seemingly invisible Body, let us have faith that it is present as the *only* Body.

Jesus had something to say to Thomas about this apparently invisible Body. You will recall that Jesus had to permit Thomas to examine the so-called visible wounded hands and his apparently sword-pierced side. It was not until then that Thomas would actually believe—have faith in the fact—that Jesus himself stood before him. When Thomas was convinced of the Presence of this eternal One by the visible evidence of something in which he could believe or have faith in, Jesus gently rebuked him:

> Jesus saith unto him, Thomas, because thou hast seen me, thou hast believed: Blessed are they that have not seen, and yet have believed (John 20:29).

Indeed, blessed are we when, even though the eternal, perfect Body seems to be invisible, we can still have absolute faith that *this Body is present and that it is the only Body that does exist right here and right now.*

Oh, it is easy to have faith in that which seems to be visible. It is easy to accept and to believe that which seems to be based upon so-called visible evidence. But it requires great courage to stand firmly in our Absolute faith when things that are supposedly seen appear to be sick or in danger. Nonetheless, it is this kind of faith that is Power.

The indwelling, all-dwelling, indivisible, seemingly invisible Presence is the Christ-Consciousness, and the ever-living Christ is the Presence of eternal, uninterrupted Perfection. The seemingly visible Body of Jesus was necessary to his fulfillment of purpose. Wasn't it necessary that he even show what appeared to be wounded matter to Thomas? Didn't even this loving, purposeful act of Jesus fulfill its purpose?

Of course, in one sense, Jesus would not have had to show Thomas any evidence of nail or spear wounds. He well knew that the Substance of his eternal, perfect Body was never nailed to a cross, nor was It ever pierced by a sword. But it did seem necessary that Thomas see something that would convince him that Life is eternal and that the Body is indestructible and imperishable. Oh, there are many Truths to be perceived as we contemplate this episode. Let us consider just a few of them.

First, the invisible Christ really is the Essence and the Activity of the Body. Again and again, Jesus, the Christ, has been referred to as the Master. Well, the Christ *is* the Master. This is true because the

Christ is the only Presence and thus the only Power. This omnipresent Christ-Power is not a Power *over* anything or anyone. There can be no "other," for the Christ is inseparably *One*. Thus, the Christ, or the Master, is not a Power over anything or anyone. But the Christ *is* Power. The Christ is the Master.

What is this Power? It is the Power of being and evidencing just what It eternally, constantly *is*. But this is not all. This Christ-presence is the Power *visibly* manifesting the Perfection It is, whenever by so doing It fulfills a purpose. This is why Jesus appeared as a perfect, visible Body. This is why he was able to show Thomas an apparently injured hand and side.

Sometimes there is a tendency to believe that the Christ began with the advent of the appearance of Jesus. This is not true. The eternal Christ *is*, and this ever-living Christ has been evidenced in what the world calls healing, or miracles, throughout the ages. In the Old Testament, supposedly concerning events before ever Jesus appeared, there are many evidences of this omnipresent Christ-Power.

In the fifth chapter of 2 Kings, we read about the so-called healing of Naaman, the leper. Now, when Naaman was cleansed, or freed, of the universal miasma, this so-called healing was evidenced as that which is called the body of flesh. "And his flesh came again like unto the flesh of a little child, and he was clean" (2 Kings 5:14). Well, this is quite visible evidence, isn't it?

Whenever Jesus performed his so-called miracles, the evidence was certainly visible. And right today, whenever a so-called healing of the visible body takes place, it is evident as the visible, perfect Body.

Now, please do not misunderstand what is being said here. We are not pretending that Spirit, Consciousness, is matter. We must reiterate: *there is no matter*. But we *must* stop this thing of knowing the Truth and then waiting for the evidence of the Truth we know. All too often, it has seemed that the evidence was not forthcoming. But enough of that. Suffice it to say that the visible evidence of the Truth, or the Presence of the Christ, does appear, and this Presence appears in tangible form. If there were no evidence, we would not be aware of the glorious fact that the omnipotent Christ is present. The evidence is tangible, but it is not material.

Now, let us clarify this statement of the fact that when a so-called healing takes place, it is evident as a visible Body. To whom is this evidence visible? To the one who appeared to be healed and to all who see—perceive—that something that had appeared to be visibly imperfect became visibly perfect. Did any change actually take place? Was there anything different in, on, or as the Substance of the one who seemed to be healed? No! Then what did take place? What did change? Ah, here is the secret! It was the *appearance* that changed. In what way did it change? *It disappeared.*

All there was to it, or of it, in the first place was an appearance. Never was it Substance, Life, Consciousness. Never was it the Christ, or God. So never did it actually exist. It only *appeared* to exist, and the ever-perfect, ever-present Christ-Consciousness—the Master—was and is the Presence of the Power that disperses the false appearance. Thus, the miasmic appearance of imperfection that seemed to be visible disappeared, revealing the ever-present Perfection, and it was and *is* this Perfection which is visible. Visible to whom? To you, to me, to all.

Now, when the imperfect appearance—leprosy—disappeared, the Body of Naaman was still visible. Furthermore, it was visible as a Body that was perfect, pure, clean "as the flesh of a little child." (Incidentally, I have seen this evidence of fresh, childlike flesh where some seemingly destructive appearance had certainly seemed to be present, and it truly is a beautiful experience.) But to continue: any appearance of imperfection is just that—an appearance—and nothing else. This is why it can and *must* disappear.

The appearance of imperfection does not change the perfect Body by one iota. This ever-perfect Body remains intact. Every aspect of this perfect Body is eternally immune to any appearance of imperfection. The *appearance* of imperfection disappears, revealing nothing other than the perfect Substance in Form, which was always all that existed as that Body. It is this eternal, perfect Substance in Form that is constantly and eternally immune to any appearance of imperfection.

Now, let us discuss further that which has been called a visible body. It is well known that even humanly no two—if there were two—of us see anything in exactly the same way. For instance, a geologist would view the Grand Canyon of Arizona from the standpoint of his particular knowledge and viewpoint of geology. A botanist would view it from his standpoint. I have never heard any two descriptions of the Grand Canyon that were exactly alike. Why? Because each one of us sees this glorious Existent from his own standpoint at the moment.

When a so-called materialist views this indescribable Beauty, he will see it as visible bigness, color, rocks, and the like. When one who is still seemingly in the grip of duality views this Grandeur, he will no doubt see it as something outside of, or other than, himself. But when an illumined one stands in awe, really seeing this Presence, he is aware of *being* all of the Perfection, the Eternality, the Bigness, the immeasurable, boundless Greatness that is evidenced right where he is. You see, as illumined Beings, we know that anything that is really evidenced right *where* we are is present and evidenced as *what* we are.

Perhaps that which has just now been said will help to clarify how it is that the Body of Perfection can be—and is—visible to one identity as an imperfect body that appears to be material. But to an illumined one, this very same Body will be tangibly revealed as all the Perfection It is, right here and right now. He will actually see It, but It will not appear to be matter. He will see It as It genuinely *is*, and thus, he will see the inherent, eternal Perfection that is ever intact and uninvaded by any appearance of imperfection. But this is not all; he will perceive that the Substance of this Body is inseparable, indivisible Consciousness. Thus, he will see that he is the Substance that is this Body, even as the Substance of this Body is the Substance, Consciousness, that he is:

> For he is our peace, who hath made both one, and hath broken down the middle wall of partition between us (Eph. 2:14).

To one who seems to be in ignorance—darkness—the Body will appear to consist of density, darkness, solidity, or matter. To one who is perhaps more knowledgeable—enlightened—the Body will appear to be a combination of soul, spirit, and matter. Also, it will seem to be comprised of a substance that is separate from, and other than, the substance that he is. But to an illumined one, the Body he sees is entirely Light, Soul, eternal, perfect, living, conscious Mind. And the illumined One will know that there is no "otherness."

This is the disappearance of that so-called "middle wall of partition between us" that is mentioned in Ephesians. The illumined Consciousness *knows* what It is seeing. If the Consciousness seems to be only partially enlightened, or awakened, there will be very little genuine knowledge of that which he sees. But to one who still seems to be in Stygian darkness—ignorance—there can be no genuine knowledge of that which he sees.

This, beloved, is why, to some of us, the Body we see appears so different from that eternal Perfection It genuinely is. But never mind; all of us must come into an awareness of "the fullness of the Godhead bodily" (Col. 2:9). Yes, all of us must completely awaken from the dreamlike *appearance* called matter, which is actually but a seeming unawareness of the genuine and *only* Body in Existence.

Now, what is the darkness—ignorance, absence of knowledge—that sees darkness or an appearance of matter? Isn't it the very same simulated, fraudulent mind that constitutes the entire illusory picture? Of course it is. So now we must perceive that actually *no one really sees matter because there is no such substance to see.*

> There is no matter, and there is no one who is aware of matter. The illusion of matter and the illusion of a mind that is aware of matter are the same illusion. Thus, when it seems that we see—or are aware of—matter, we are actually no one seeing nothing.

This does not mean, however, that there is no visible Body. What it does mean is that this Body right here *is* visible to the Vision of one who knows what constitutes the Substance in Form that he is seeing. But we must consider a further aspect of this Truth.

For instance, how can it be possible for so-called "others" who are not enlightened to see the evidence of Perfection, called healing, when imperfection has apparently disappeared? The answer to this question has to do with Consciousness. When a so-called healing takes place, the one who seems to be healed is aware of the disappearance of an imperfect appearance, and he is also aware of, or conscious of, the evidence of Perfection right where imperfection had seemed to be.

Now, we have so often said that "our Consciousness is our Universe." Well, our Consciousness is our Body. Whatever we are conscious of, we are conscious of being. When one is conscious of Perfection, he is conscious of being perfect; thus, he is conscious *of* a perfect Body. But he is also conscious of *being* a perfect Body. This one's awareness of having realized his Perfection would have to be the awareness of everyone he knew. It would be the Consciousness of all those called "others," because there is one indivisible Consciousness. This being true, his very awareness of himself as being perfect would also be their awareness of him as being perfect.

In other words, what we see and know our Self to be is seen and known by all of those called "others." But it is necessary to realize the inseparable Nature of all Consciousness in order to perceive this very profound Truth. Now you can see just why the revelation of inseparability is so vitally important.

Beloved, in the first volume of this classwork, we promised that we would reveal the way in which this Absolute Truth is evidenced in and as our daily living and as our Body. In the foregoing revelations, we feel that a seeming gap has been closed — or the middle wall of partition dissolved — between our perception of the Body and the evidence of this perception as the tangibly perfect Body.

From the foregoing, you will perceive that "the fullness of the Godhead bodily" really means that the Body really is the completeness of the Mind, Consciousness, Life, Love that is God. The "Godhead" signifies the conscious, Universal Mind — Intelligence — which is God. The "fullness" is the completeness of all that universal, living, conscious Mind is and knows Itself to be. "Bodily," of course, signifies that God — *as All that God is* — really is all there is of this Body right here and right now.

Once the misconception — appearance of darkness, density, ignorance — is completely obliterated, this Body is visible, and It is the *only* Body that can be seen or known. Indeed, there is no "other" to see or to know.

It is true — your Consciousness *is* your Universe. But it is also true that your Consciousness is your Body. God, Universal Consciousness, is complete as your Body. This God-Consciousness is your very awareness that you exist. It is your Universal

Identity. It is your specific Identity. What you are conscious of *being* is the Substance, Form, and Activity of your Body.

> What you are conscious of being is seen and is known by those called "others" because the Consciousness you are, knowing what you are, is the Consciousness of everyone.

This is why they must—and do—see the Perfection that you know your Self to be. Since *you* know it, the only Mind, or Consciousness, that exists as your Universe *has* to know it.

This is the Power of your knowing. You can see that it is not a power *over* anyone or anything. Rather, it is simply that in-dwelling, all-dwelling, indivisible Christ—the Master—aware of being the Perfection that It eternally is. It is the Power of "being" rather than the power of "doing." It is the Power of being the Truth you know rather than an assumptive power of knowing the Truth *about* your Self or anyone.

Jesus has said, "And I, if I be lifted up from the earth, will draw all men unto me" (John 12:32). Yes, as the Consciousness that you are is uplifted far beyond the simulated mirage of appearance, all men will perceive the Truth that you are, but they will also perceive that they are this same Truth.

This, Beloved, is seeing and being the Light. Let your Light shine because you really are the Light to the assumptive world of appearance. You can see that it is all a matter of Consciousness, your Consciousness, aware of being what you are. This is that which reveals the Perfection that you are to, and as, your Self, and this Self knowing is what reveals the Perfection you are to everyone — yes, even *as* the Consciousness of everyone. But greater still is the fact that this Self knowing is what reveals the Perfection that everyone really is. It can be no other way because, you see, there is no division, no separation at all, in or as the conscious, loving, living Mind that you are.

All Truth — all that is true — is perfect and eternal. There can be no imperfect Truth. Neither can there be a temporal Truth. You *are* the Truth. You are that which is perfect and eternally true. Yet *the power of this glorious fact rests entirely in your awareness of being this Truth.*

It does not help very much for you to be perfect and eternal unless you are aware or conscious of being what you are. You see, this Universe is comprised of God conscious of being what God *is.* Thus you, in order to be the evidence of what you are, must of necessity be comprised of the God-Consciousness that you are, *knowing what you are.* It is in the knowing of what you are that the evidence of what you are is apparent. This is the Power. This is the in-dwelling, all-dwelling, indivisible Christ — God — Consciousness that you are, knowing what you are and *evidencing* what you know.

It is the evidence of what you know, and know your Self to be, that fulfills the purpose of your knowing. Just to know the Truth is never sufficient. In order to be the actual evidence of the Truth, it is necessary to know that *you are this very Truth you know*. In short, you are your own evidence of the Truth you know and know your Self to be. But in order to be this evidence, it is necessary to know that *you are It*, here, now, eternally. In this way, the perfect, eternal Truth you know your Self to be is evident as the perfect, eternal Body that you are aware of being. Also, in this way, your eternal, perfect Body fulfills Its purpose in being your Body.

Never doubt but that the Body exists as the fulfillment of a specific purpose. In the first volume of this classwork, it was revealed that the Body is necessary to your completeness as well as to the completeness of the Universe. That which is essential to your completeness is also essential to your complete fulfillment of purpose. The eternal Identity necessitates an eternal Body. Why? *Because eternally you are the fulfillment of a specific, as well as a universal, purpose.*

In order to *be* the fulfillment of Its eternal purpose in being, this Body must be a good and perfect Body. In fact, It has to be so eternally durable that It can never wear out or run down. This glorious Body consists of the changeless Essence which comprises this eternal Universe, and the Universe is very durable indeed. It has to be durable in order to be an eternal Universe. Never limit the Body and Its eternal durability, imperishability, indestructibility.

It is true that this Body is but an infinitesimal focal point of the Universal Entirety which is the Body of the Universe. Yet if *this* Body were to be an imperfect body, the Body—without circumference—of the Universe, God, would not be perfect. In order for anything to be perfect, it has to be completely perfect. If there should be the slightest flaw, there could not be Perfection.

Now, we know that this boundless, immeasurable Universe is God, and God is Perfection Itself. In order that the Perfection which is God be eternally and constantly perfect, every iota of this Allness has to be completely and eternally perfect. There cannot be even so much as a minute focal point that is not eternally, completely perfect. This Body is the inseparable, perfect All. It *has* to be the Perfection that is the eternal, perfect All. And it *is*.

Perhaps one of the most tragic illusions of all the simulated mirage is that called "old age." First it *seems* that the Body begins to change, to run down, become inadequate, etc. Then it sometimes appears that the mind can become hazy or unintelligent. Oh, why talk about all this miasma? We already know too much about these fictitious appearances called old age. Let us perceive just why these fallacies seem to be so prevalent, and then let us perceive how this whole miasma may be transcended.

If there were such a thing as old age, it would have to begin at birth. The very moment a supposedly new body is seemingly born, the illusion of age begins. Anything that can begin, as something new, must get old and appear to go through all the process of aging. It is the body that is supposed to be born, to sicken, to age, and to die.

Therefore, we realize that birth can only *seem* to be because a supposedly born or new body *appears* to become evident. In order to completely transcend the whole fraudulent illusion of age, we must perceive the Absolute Truth: *there is no birth.* Yes, there is no born or created body. There is no "becoming." All is constant and complete. There is no becoming, either new or old.

Beloved, there are many seeming inharmonies in what appears as our human experience, in which it is necessary to perceive the fact that eternal, immutable, living, conscious Mind is never born. But when we seem to be faced with what the world calls old age or death, it is of the utmost importance that we perceive the birthless, ageless, deathless Nature of the Identity and *particularly of the Body.*

We know that virtually every living thing seems to have to be born, or to become a *new* existent, in one way or another. The seed is supposed to produce the new tree; the egg is believed to produce the new bird. All about us, there does appear to be evidence of a supposedly newborn life, or a newborn body. It is no simple matter to refuse to believe this utterly false evidence. Nonetheless, our perception of the Absolute Fact that *any* evidence of birth or of a newborn body is completely fraudulent, obliterates this fallacious evidence. We will never stop this tragic appearance of old age, deterioration, and death until we stop giving any credence whatever to birth.

All the seeming problems of so-called human life stem from the illusion that we were born as a new material body, and thus we began to experience the things of a material world. It is this fallacy of a supposedly "new" body that appears to become an "old" body. It is this same illusory falsification that presents distorted pictures all during our so-called human life. It also can seem to present distorted and troublesome experiences, and these illusory experiences can range all the way from fear through sorrow, heartbreak, resentment, and all that is supposed to make up a temporary life.

All there is to an appearance of old age is an illusion of accumulated human experiences, and this accumulation of so-called human experiences is supposed to *begin* with birth. Is it any wonder that we say, "Birth is the beginning of death"? Actually, there will come a day when we will realize that what we call birth is the only death there is. (But really, there is neither birth nor death. Neither is there a period of time between birth and death. There is no time for either, for there is no time.)

All that is called "memory" has to do with these same illusions. We seem to accumulate memories of incidents, events, poor health, good health, sorrow, joy, etc., that are supposed to have happened since "birth." Have you ever noticed that one of the first signs of the illusion that one is becoming older is that he or she begins to talk much about the past? And it is noteworthy that many of those who *appear* to be aged literally live in the past. This is all part and parcel of the illusion that birth really does take place and that a new mind and a new body has come into being. Naturally, if the foregoing were true, this "new mind" would become an "old mind," and the "new body" would inevitably become an "old body."

Please be assured that we do not wish to speak of these illusions. We know that they are entirely fraudulent appearances, but we also know that these appearances must be faced and seen through. We can't hide our heads in the sand and just pretend that (if we don't look) they will go away. We must face these falsifications squarely, and we must go all the way in our perception of that which *is* true rather than of that which *appears* to be true—*and is not.*

We know that a mirage may present a false picture of a lake, and this apparent lake may be right in the path of our car. We know we are going to have to come to this supposed lake. We don't stop the car. We don't turn around and go back, and neither do we take a detour. We face this mirage that seems to be a lake. We drive right up to it. And when we have firmly faced it and gone right up to it, we find that there is no lake at all. In fact, there is not so much as a drop of water in our path. But best of all, we know that *never was there a lake there.*

The foregoing is but a simile, but it serves to illustrate the absolute nothingness of memory and old age. It is necessary to face these falsifications and recognize that they are nothing but mirages, illusions, with no substance, activity, form, or life.

There is no such thing as babyhood, childhood, youth, middle age, or old age. *There is no age.* This is a word that should be omitted from our vocabulary, *and it would be well to omit it right now.* Oh, it is being discovered that things are not the way they seem to be.

For instance, recently I have learned that the Eastman Kodak Company, in collaboration with another large corporation, has now a marvelous process of photography. In this process, they can photograph the bud of a rose, but the finished photograph shows the full-blown rose rather than the bud. This alone should mean much to us. It is at least some proof that nothing comes into being, nothing goes out of being. One day, they will be able to take a picture of a seemingly withered rose, and this picture will still show the ever perfect, ever fresh and new, full-blown, beautiful rose. Let us consider just what this means, and all that it means, in our contemplation.

It means that right where the baby body appears to be, there is the eternal Body, which is forever at the very peak of Its completeness in every way. It means that right where it seems there is an aging or aged body, there is the eternal Body which can never be less—or other—than the eternal Body which remains forever at the very peak of Its perfection, freshness, and newness. It means that right here and right now, the Body you have—and are—is gloriously perfect, new, and fresh, constantly and without interruption.

Sometimes, when we are in illumination, we see the Body. It may be the Body of a so-called infant or the Body of one who seems to be mature or perhaps aging or aged. No matter how this body that we see may *appear* to be to the unillumined sense, in illumination we always see the perfect Body at the very peak of Its perfection. I have never seen a baby body, a child body, an aging or aged body when I was in illumination. Always, illumined Consciousness reveals the eternal, immutable Body, and always It is revealed as It is. Never is It revealed as immature or past maturity. It makes no difference whether or not the Body I see is supposed to be the Body of a baby, a child, or of one who is supposed to be aged. In illumination, we see the Body as It eternally *is*.

Many so-called healings have taken place when suddenly the Body of the one who has asked for help appears right within and as the Consciousness, and this Body is perceived in all Its wonderful Perfection and Beauty. Of course, I never try to visualize the Body. To do anything as foolish as that would be diametrically opposite to the basic premise of the Ultimate. It is just that someone who has called for help will suddenly be visible. There is nothing supernatural or mysterious about this experience. I don't regard it as a mystical experience. It is all normal and natural. And the wonderful aspect of this experience is that generally when this takes place, there is what the world of appearance calls a healing.

This brings us to an important aspect of our fulfillment of purpose. Whenever we contemplate, it is well to realize that our contemplation is the fulfillment of a glorious purpose. This does not mean that we contemplate with an objective in Consciousness. We do not contemplate for the purpose of accomplishing something or of changing something. We do not contemplate from the standpoint of the fallacy that some purpose will be fulfilled through our contemplation. Rather, we contemplate knowing that *every purpose is constantly fulfilled and that our contemplation is merely the consideration of this fact*. Fulfillment of purpose does not mean that there is an unfulfilled purpose. Rather, it means that we are the constant fulfillment of whatever our purpose is at the moment.

There is quite a difference in contemplating for the purpose of accomplishing something and contemplating for the sheer joy of perceiving that every purpose, or even some specific purpose, is constantly and eternally fulfilled. In this way, we realize that our contemplation is the omniactive Mind which is God in action, constantly fulfilling Its purpose in being and in being Omniaction. Above all, we contemplate in the full awareness that everything already *is* and every activity is already going on.

Now let us continue with our consideration of the eternal, perfect Body. We know that the Body consists of eternal, perfect, living, intelligent, loving Consciousness. We also know that It exists as the fulfillment of a universal, as well as a specific, purpose. But perhaps we wonder about those aspects of the Body that are called organs, cells, atoms, etc. We may wonder about their activity and whether this activity is also a fulfillment of purpose.

All activity is the fulfillment of purpose. This is why there is activity. This is why God is Omniaction, everywhere and eternally.

Let us speak briefly about the aspects of the Body called organs, cells, atoms, etc. There is absolutely nothing that is material existing as this Body. It is exceedingly necessary to be constantly aware of this fact, Let us not delve into these aspects of the Body as though we were seeking some so-called human explanation of their existence. The best way to contemplate the Completeness that is the

Body is the way we contemplate the boundless Body of the Universe—God.

We know that the universal Body consists of an infinite variety of aspects of Itself. Let us call these necessary aspects members of the Universal Body. Every aspect, every member of the Universal Body, is necessary to the Completeness that is this glorious, perfect Body of God. Every member of this Body is active, and it is actively, perfectly, intelligently fulfilling its purpose in being.

Witness the perfect, surging, flowing, orderly, irresistible, unobstructed activity of the stars and planets and of this earth planet. All of these exist as members of the Universal Body.

Now, this specific Body also exists as an infinite variety of aspects of the Universal Body and *an infinite variety of aspects of Itself.* Every aspect of this Body is necessary to Its completeness. The perfect, irresistible, irrepressible activity of every aspect of this Body is necessary to Its eternality, to Its constant perfection, and to Its perfect fulfillment of purpose. It is necessary to perceive that this Body does not consist of a substance or an activity separate from, or other than, the Substance and Its activity which comprise the Universal Body. Neither is It separated from the Universal Body you are by Its outline or delineation. Your Universal Consciousness is the Universal Body that you are.

With the foregoing clearly established in and as our Consciousness, we can now perceive that which is necessary to the completeness of this specific Body. And we certainly know there are *no* material organs, cells, etc. This specific Body is complete. Its eternal, immutable, perfect Completeness necessitates the presence of every so-called atom and item that is necessary to Its completeness. It makes no difference what the fraudulent world of sense calls the organs, atoms, cells, etc. They do exist *as what they are*. They do exist as the fulfillment of a specific, as well as a universal, purpose.

Furthermore, their perfect activity is irresistible and irrepressible. It is absolutely necessary to the universal fulfillment of purpose, and this activity is also necessary to the specific fulfillment of purpose of this Body right here and now. Perfect Omniaction is continuous in and as *all* the activity of every so-called member of this Body. If this were not true, this Body could not be an eternal, perfect Body, and thus, the Universal Body—that you eternally and infinitely are—could not be a perfect, eternal Body.

All that is necessary for the completeness and the complete fulfillment of the purpose of this Body exists in and as the Body. Nothing exists within or as this Body that is not necessary to Its eternal perfection and to Its eternal, complete fulfillment of purpose. All the activity that is necessary to the ever-newness of this Body is going on here and now. It is perfect activity, with no cessation or variation, because it is Mind—your infinite Intelligence—in action. It matters not whether it is called the activity of the heart, the head, the stomach, or whatever; it is all the Substance which is your Consciousness actively fulfilling Its purpose in being.

The purpose that is fulfilled as the entirety of this specific Body is identically the same purpose that is eternally fulfilled as your Universal Body. What is this purpose? It is the eternal maintenance of the Universal You, I, All, as immutable, perfect, conscious, intelligent, living Love. This, Beloved, is the Body you are. This is the Body you have always been and will forever be.

Now that we know what the Body is, why It is necessary, and the Universal—as well as the specific—purpose that It fulfills, let us briefly discuss a question that is often asked: "What is the spiritual significance of food, water, etc.?"

Food and water are no more material than is the Body. Thus, we do not actually partake of material food or liquid. The essence of food and liquid is Consciousness—your Consciousness—which is not contained or confined within the delineation of your Body. You do not take anything *into* the Body from *outside* your Consciousness, which is the Essence of the Body. There is no "outside." Nonetheless, there is a very significant Truth that is signified by that which is called eating and drinking.

We know that food and liquid are supposed to be necessary to the maintenance and the sustenance of the body. It is also generally believed that food and liquid provide strength, energy, and vitality that are necessary for the perfect functioning of the body. It is even said that without water or liquid the body would not survive very long and that the continuance of life is dependent upon food and liquid.

Now, of course, all of this is in the illusory realm of the fraudulent appearance of body. Nonetheless, it does signify the Presence of Absolute Truth. It does signify the Presence of the fulfillment of purpose which is called food and liquid.

The Absolute Truth signified by the foregoing is the constant, eternal maintenance and sustenance of the Body. It is this constant maintenance of this Body that is evidenced as Its ever new, fresh, perfect Substance. Then, too, there is activity signified by that which is called eating and drinking, and this activity *seems* to be human in its nature. But this is not true. Rather, it is omniactive Mind in action. Infinite Mind is active as the fulfillment of Its purpose, and It does fulfill Its purpose in being this specific activity.

It is well known that all activity is circular in its movement. It has been said that there are no straight lines in nature. There are many evidences of the fact that Omniaction is circular, specifically and universally. The movement of all stars and planets, the galaxies, etc., is circular. All of us know that the Body is said to have a circulatory system. Well, the partaking, digesting, and eliminating of food and liquid signifies this universal, as well as specific, surging, circular Omniaction. This is why there is such irrepressible, perfect activity constantly going on in and as the Body.

The so-called bodily activity really is the Universal Omniaction fulfilling Its purpose as the bodily activity. What exists that can obstruct It? What exists that can interfere with It? What exists that can resist It, slow It down, or speed It up? Eternally, this omnipotent Omniaction goes on. It is never interrupted. It never begins and It never ends. It fulfills Its purpose of being Life Itself. It fulfills Its purpose by being eternal, perfect, omniactive, intelligent, loving, conscious Life.

It is necessary for us to *know* what comprises the Body and Its purpose in being. It is also essential that we know the Universal Nature of the bodily activity. We must know that the Body, as well as the bodily activity, exists eternally as the fulfillment of a universal, as well as a specific, purpose. All of this we must know. Why? Because the Body and the bodily activity consist of the forever living, conscious Mind that we are. In short, the Body consists of the Mind we are, knowing the Truth we know. If we know the Truth that *is* the Body, this Body evidences the Truth we know. It has to be this evidence because It is the very presence of the conscious, living Mind that we are, knowing what we are.

We have gone quite thoroughly into this subject of Body because we realize that the Body is that aspect of Being that seems most difficult to understand. The Bible states that death is the last enemy to be overcome—seen through—and this is true because it is the misconception of body that seems to be born and thus seems to die. As stated before, we must be through with the appearance of death, and we will be free of this so-called last enemy by a complete, full knowledge of that which comprises the eternal Body of Light, Consciousness. We will also perceive the impossibility of death as we perceive that the Body exists as an eternal fulfillment of purpose.

Beloved, that which immediately follows is of the utmost importance, and I cannot tell you—in words—how necessary it is for you to thoroughly study and contemplate the following statements. It will be most helpful if you will frequently read, study, and contemplate that which follows.

> We realize now why it is necessary to know what the Body is and why It exists. But it is equally important and necessary that we maintain our universal perspective once we really know what—and why—the Body exists.

> It is better to give as little attention to It as possible. Consider It in and as Its proper existence and fulfillment of purpose in and as your universal Existence. Give It Its proper role in and as your daily living, but don't over-emphasize It. Don't constantly focus your attention on or as the body. Don't consider It to be more important than is any other aspect of your Universal Self. Don't consider It to be any more important than are the everyday aspects of your business, your profession, employment, or whatever.

It is sufficient just to know what It is and why It is what It is. If It seems to need any attention, you may rest assured that you will know it. Other than that, it is better to give It as little attention—consideration—as possible. In other words, maintain a balanced perspective of the Body.

Let us explain just why it is so important that we keep our perspective where the Body is concerned. In the fraudulent world of appearance, the body seems to *demand* too much attention. It appears to constantly make demands that focus the attention upon it. It may all too frequently demand food or drink. It may make demands upon us that would be considered even harmful or, at least, unnecessary. It may seem to demand attention because it appears to ache, to pain, to be swollen, inflamed, infected, or whatever.

In any event, this wholly fictitious sense of body does seem to insist upon our attention, and thus we seem to be out of balance, to lose our perspective. This is a balanced Universe, and our attention must be a perfectly balanced attention. Everything is in perfect balance and order. It is necessary that we maintain a well-balanced perspective in *all* our daily living.

In the foregoing paragraph, we have spoken of the body as it *seems* to be and is not. However, it is well to recognize this illusory trap concerning the body and to refuse to become enmeshed in its pretenses. Certain it is that our clear perception of Body should not mean a loss of perspective where the Body is concerned. Although the Body is an important aspect of our Being, we do not give undue emphasis to this specific aspect. Actually, we do not emphasize any particular aspect of our Being. Oh, sometimes it does seem necessary for us to focus our attention specifically upon one or another aspect of our Existence, but we find that there is an overall balance in all of our contemplative perception.

All of us have observed those who seemed to be over-concerned with one particular aspect of their Existence. We have also noticed that this undue concern seemed to limit them in many ways. Sometimes one may be overly concerned with business to the point that the home is neglected. Again, one may be so concerned with the home that this imbalance limits the overall activity in and as other aspects of fulfillment of purpose. Sometimes the seeming imbalance may be an over-emphasis about money, health, pleasure, or clothes.

Oh, there are innumerable ways in which we can *seem* to limit our Self. One of the more subtle aspects of this seeming imbalance has to do with one specific Identity. It may appear that the attention is focused almost entirely upon one Identity and that no one and nothing is important but this one Identity. This is indeed duality. Here again, there seems to be great limitation. We could go on indefinitely with these fallacious examples, but it is not necessary. It is sufficient that we remain alert to these pretensions.

Let us now continue with our discussion pertaining to the most prevalent aspect of this seeming imbalance. This, of course, is the Body. As stated before, the Body is but an infinitesimal focal point in the infinite Identity that you are. And the Power that you are is the infinite, or Universal, *I* that you are. You know that the Universe is your boundless, Universal Body.

Those of us who experience full illumination *know* that we are the Entirety that is this Universe. It is seeing universally and being all that we see. It is an awareness of *being* the Substance, Form, and Activity of every sun, moon, star, and planet. It is an awareness of being everywhere because *we are the Everywhere.* In this illumination, we can clearly see that this Earth Planet is but a tiny focal point of the universal Completeness we know our Self to be.

Knowing that we are *the Everywhere,* our attention may be focused at any point, or aspect, of the Universal All that we are aware of being. It is impossible to describe this illumined experience, but it is possible to say that we may be aware that we are focused anywhere. It is never a matter of projecting the Self to a given point; rather, it is simply an awareness of *being* present at that focal point. To us, no matter where we find our Self, that focal point is *here.*

In this realization, we perceive that there is no "there." Everywhere is *here,* and we are the *here* that is the Everywhere. It is in this boundless awareness of Being that we perceive the utter futility of any fallacious sense of limitation. Our perspective is limitless, boundless, and immeasurable.

Beloved, I have spoken of this illumination for the fulfillment of a definite purpose, and this purpose is your realization of the boundless, eternal, immeasurable Nature of your Being. It is true that, for the moment, you may seem to be fulfilling but a limited purpose and in a very small area. But this is only the way it appears.

Oh, you are so big, so boundless, that there is no way to measure the greatness that you are or that your fulfillment of purpose is, right this moment.

Never limit your Self. It is in your awareness of being boundless and immeasurable that you realize this perfect order, perfect balance, and limitless perspective that is essential to your Completeness.

If you should permit your attention to be focused almost constantly on *any* aspect of your Existence, it would seem to limit your boundless perspective. It would also be dualistic. This is particularly true of the Body because it is the Body that seems to limit us to such a small perspective of our immeasurable Self. As we have said, the Body is but a pinpoint in the Universal Consciousness that is your Entirety.

We cannot separate the activity of the Body from our activity in the home, in our business, in our profession, or in any aspect of our everyday experience. The conscious, loving, living Mind that is active as the activity of the Body is the very same Mind that is active as our home affairs, our business or professional living, or whatever. There is nothing that can separate Consciousness, *and the conscious, living Mind that is active as one aspect of Itself, is equally active as every aspect of Itself.* It is in this way that infinite Mind fulfills Its universal purpose, as well as Its specific purpose, and this is the Mind that you are.

It may appear that the covering of the Body, called skin, acts as a container or confiner of the conscious, living Mind that you are. There is *nothing* solid, hard, or resistant in this Universe.

Jesus well knew this to be true. He knew that so-called solid walls could not exclude him from the room where the disciples were, and he also knew that those seemingly solid walls could not confine him. Furthermore, he evidenced this very fact. (Incidentally, today there are many who are evidencing this same fact, and this has nothing to do with spiritualism at all. Neither is it mysterious or supernatural.)

Our point is that the Consciousness that *you* are is unconfined. Certain it is that the Body or Its covering does not confine your limitless Consciousness within the Body. Neither does It limit this Consciousness to what would be called your immediate environment. Now you can perceive how it is and why it is that your activity in the home or in the business world is identically the same activity, whether it is called business activity or bodily activity.

Suppose that you were successfully employed in a large, busy office. Suppose that it seemed some aspect of your Body was not functioning perfectly. Should your attention be focused entirely upon the Body or upon the activity of one aspect of the Body? No. Rather, you would be aware of the fact that the very same conscious Intelligence in action that was apparent as the activity of your Body was also evident as the perfect, intelligent activity of the office and of every Identity that was engaged in that office activity.

This is a very small example of the tremendous importance of being limitless and boundless in your contemplations. Of course, you would not limit your awareness of being this boundless activity to just the office. You would also perceive that this omniactive Consciousness that you are is evident as everyone who walks, talks, drives a car, or whatever.

Oh, there are no limits to the ways in which the evidence of your indivisible, conscious, living Mind may be—and is—evidenced. Perhaps, though, the foregoing similes will provide a basis for your further contemplation of this fact.

Chapter X

Vision

Vision is one of the most important aspects of our entire Being. No doubt this is true because we seem to base our judgment—or opinions—upon that which we seem to see. This may explain why it is that so-called problems concerning Vision appear to be so prevalent.

What is Vision? Vision is conscious perception, or Consciousness perceiving. *It is Consciousness distinguishing distinct aspects of Itself.* If you were unconscious—which is impossible—you would see nothing, even though you were supposed to have perfect Vision.

There is one Vision and One who has Vision. This is the Consciousness that *is* Vision. No one can possess Vision. No one can be dispossessed of Vision. It is indivisible, inseparable, and It is equally present everywhere and eternally. It can never be diminished. Neither can It be augmented. It is an omnipresent, eternal, perfect Constant. Vision is a Universal Fact, or Truth, and *you are this Truth.*

> Perfect vision is the single eye which sees things as they are. It is perfect Consciousness perceiving Perfection.

Now, we have stated just what Universal Vision—the Vision you *are*—really is. Let us bring this glorious, unlimited perception to the specific aspect of your Universal Vision, which fulfills Its purpose as your Vision right here and now. (Of course, you know it is the Vision that you *are* and not a Vision you possess.) Nonetheless, Vision exists as the fulfillment of a specific purpose as well as the fulfillment of a Universal purpose. So let us be specific in our consideration of this aspect of our Existence.

The purpose of Vision is to see. Vision fulfills Its purpose by seeing. Perfect Vision fulfills Its purpose by seeing perfectly, right here and right now. The eyes are supposed to be the avenue, or instrument, through which we see. This is not true. The eyes are not vehicles or instruments through which Vision filters. Rather, the eyes are the Vision Itself. Let us see how this can be true.

The Substance of the Eyes is Consciousness. The purpose of Consciousness is to be conscious, to perceive. Thus, the very Substance of the Eyes is the Consciousness that perceives, or sees. You can be sure that the purpose of the Eyes is to see. It is to distinguish the various Essences and Forms in which Consciousness is evident. The Vision, which comprises the Substance called the Eyes, fulfills Its purpose in just this way. The entire Substance of the Eyes consists of the Vision—Consciousness—which sees or perceives various aspects of Substance in

Form, and it is this Vision in Form called the Eyes that distinguishes their distinction. There is distinction in and as Consciousness in Form, but there is *no* separation. Yet, to the seemingly limited human sense of vision, it *appears* that substance in form is separated into bits and parts of itself.

Of course, you realize that the Presence of Consciousness, the Substance that sees, does not exclude the Presence of Mind, Life, or Love. It is Consciousness that sees or perceives; it is Mind — Intelligence — that discriminates or makes the distinction of the so-called objects which are really aspects of what is seen. It is Life that is the activity of seeing, and it is Love that is the Perfection, the perfect harmony, of both the Vision that sees and that which is seen. Seeing as the Vision that is Love always means seeing Perfection.

As so often stated, Consciousness, Mind, Life, Love, are inseparably *One*. Thus, the Substance of the Eye that sees is living, intelligent, loving Consciousness. Life is the Activity; Mind is the Intelligence; Love is the indivisible, harmonious Oneness; Consciousness is the Essence of the eternal, perfect Vision.

Right now, there is one realization of Vision that must be clear: Vision is not confined. Rather, Vision is present as the entire Substance of the Body. The Body *is* conscious, living, intelligent Love, and this is Vision. There are authenticated cases on record, available to anyone, which prove that it is possible to "see" with the fingertips. Not long ago, it was discovered that, according to the so-called human sense, the entire face was capable of "seeing." And more recently, they have come to the conclusion that the entire chest can also "see."

Well, they are coming along, even though it appears to be "matter" seeing. One day they will discover that the entire Essence that is the Body is that which sees. It really is the Consciousness which is Vision Itself. But we know that it is the boundless, indivisible Consciousness that we *are* that "sees." We know that the purpose of Vision is to see and that there is nothing existing that can interfere with the complete fulfillment of purpose of the Vision that sees.

There is another—and exceedingly important—aspect of Vision that we should consider. This aspect is the indivisibility of the Vision that sees and of that which is seen. Vision is completely unconfined. It is no more confined to the Body than is Consciousness, for Consciousness *is* Vision. It appears that we see a tree, a rose, mountain, etc., "out there." But there is no "out there." That which we see is not separate from, or other than, our Consciousness, which *is* the Vision. So we can never view anything at a distance. The Consciousness we are is right where the tree, rose, mountain, etc., is. And moreover, *our Consciousness is the very Substance of whatever we see*. Thus, we know that the Consciousness which is the Vision is the very Substance, the Form, and the Activity of that which we see.

In this way, we can perceive that there is no far or near; there is only here. Perfect, intelligent, conscious, loving Vision sees perfectly because It *is* the Perfection that It sees, right where It is seeing; and that is right here where the attention is focused. Now we realize that Vision is not confined to the Eye, to the Body, or indeed to anything or anywhere. We are the Vision that sees; we are the Entirety of that which is seen.

All that is true as Vision is also true as hearing. Should there appear to be some problem of hearing, it would be well to contemplate what has been revealed on Vision and realize that there is no separation between Vision and hearing. Even as the Consciousness that sees is the Substance of the Eye that sees and the Substance of that which It sees, so it is that the Consciousness that hears is the Substance — Essence — of the hearing Ear and the very Essence of that which It hears.

There is one indivisible Sense, and this Sense is Consciousness, or awareness. There are distinct aspects or functions of this one Sense — Consciousness — but there is no separation. Actually, the so-called functions of Consciousness are innumerable. So, instead of five senses, we are aware of being innumerable spiritual aspects, or activities, of the One inseparable Consciousness.

Chapter XI

Immunity

There are many ways in which *apparent* inharmony can seem to invade our Consciousness as we go about our daily affairs. These appearances can certainly seem to interrupt our awareness of the Truth we know, and know our limitless Self to be. A very few examples will suffice to illustrate our point.

Perhaps someone in our office or place of employment appears to be very antagonistic, vexing, aggressive, envious, or domineering. Sometimes it seems almost impossible to maintain our clear awareness of being the Love that we are. Perhaps it may be someone in the home who apparently manifests unloving and selfish traits. It may appear that a member of the family is an alcoholic or is addicted to some other form of so-called human bondage. Perhaps it seems that all our *efforts* to see Perfection as the only Presence have seemed to avail nothing. Then we ask, "What shall I do?"

In situations such as the foregoing, you can *do* nothing. Even if you were able to, through trying or making an effort, reform a so-called imperfect Individual, he or she would inevitably slip right back into the seeming difficulty in one way or another. Yet it is unnecessary to continue indefinitely seeming to endure these appearances of selfishness, weakness, egotism, and the like. Let us perceive the way in which we can be completely immune to any appearance of this nature and the way in which even the *appearance* vanishes into its complete nothingness. In this way, the one who seemed so difficult may also be helped, even though he or she may not know from whence the help came.

The Consciousness that you are — *knowing* what you are and being what you know — is your immunity to any appearance of evil. Let us perceive how this awareness manifests itself as complete harmony in and as your office, your place of employment, your home, or whatever. Ask your Self, "What am I? What am I conscious of being? Am I conscious of selfishness, egotism, dishonesty, alcoholism, or any of these so-called human traits? If I can be *conscious of* such falsities, must I not be aware of *being* these very fallacious appearances?"

When these questions announce themselves, you immediately become aware of the following Truths:

> I know that the Consciousness I am is not one of these fallacies. I know what I am. Only that which I know am I. Only that which I know my Self to be can possibly exist in and as my daily experience. This is but another way of saying, "My Consciousness is my Universe, and my Universe is my Consciousness."

You know that there is no selfish, scheming, little assumptive identity present as the Consciousness that *you are*. Therefore, no such assumptive mind is present in or as your Universe or your daily experience. You know that there is no little egotistical mind parading around here as the Mind that *you are*; thus, there is no such mind present or active in or as your everyday experience. You know that the Consciousness that *you are* is not weak, not addicted to alcohol, or to any other apparent vices, so none of these illusions can be present in or as your Consciousness, which is your home. You know that the Consciousness *you are* is not aware of being hateful, avaricious, contrary, stubborn, or any other of these fallacies. Hence, none of these apparent traits can be present or active in or as your Existence.

How and why do you know that none of these fallacies are present as the Consciousness that *you are*? Beloved, no evil can be present in or as your Consciousness—which is your Universe—because *you know what you are, and you are what you know*. You are omnipotent, omnipresent, living, principled Love, and *you know what you are*.

This is your answer to every seeming appearance of anything that would—if it could—tempt you to accept and to seem to experience inharmony. Omnipotent, omnipresent, living, principled Love is your immunity, and *you are this Love*.

When you are engaged in your activity in the office, home, or anywhere, your attention is focused right where you are fulfilling a specific purpose at the moment. Always know that wherever and whenever the attention of your infinite Being is brought to a focal point, right then and there the full and complete Power of the universal, perfect Consciousness *you are* is present and manifested right at that focal point.

Of course, we are not speaking of a location in so-called space. Yet wherever your attention is focused, the omnipotent God-Consciousness that you are is fully and completely evidenced as Absolute Perfection. Never limit the power of your "seeing." It is God who "seeth" as you, both to will and to do of His own good pleasure. Your "seeing" is the God-Consciousness that you are, perceiving Its eternal, perfect, constant Perfection in and as every aspect of Its Being.

Does this mean that you condone that which seems to be wrong? Indeed no.

> Love is Mind — Intelligence — and intelligent
> Love acts and loves intelligently.

Never are you required to love that which appears to be evil. But neither do you condemn it as though it really existed as a person or personal evil. You do not ignore it either. Jesus did not ignore that which appeared to be evil. Rather, he had some very strong words to say when illusory evil attempted to appear as persons:

> Get thee behind me, Satan: thou art an
> offense unto me: for thou savourest not the things

that be of God, but those that be of men (Matt. 16:23).

Here, Jesus was supposed to be rebuking Peter. But Jesus did not personalize the seeming evil. He called it "Satan," not giving it a personal name. He clearly recognized that there is no personal evil. (Actually, there is no evil.) But Jesus did not ignore the mass illusion called evil. In the eighth chapter of John, Jesus used even stronger words in rebuking so-called evil. Yet he did not make his rebuke personal:

> When he speaketh a lie, he speaketh of his own; for he is a liar, and the father of lies.

We do not ignore the appearance called evil. We don't just pretend that if we can't see it, it will go away. We face this illusory mass illusion, knowing its nothingness. But we do not attach it to any individual. There is no personal evil. Actually, there is no person to be evil. We do not condone assumptive evil, and we certainly do not love it. When someone appears in or as our daily experience who *seems* to be other than the God-Consciousness that is the *only* Identity, our reaction is to love the God-Consciousness but not the appearance of evil. How shall we perceive the Truth in a situation where selfishness, ego, weakness, seem to be present as an individual? We simply see universal, impersonal, inseparable, Life, Mind, Consciousness, Love, and we do not even see an individual.

We do not look at (or consider) a seemingly imperfect individual and try to see this one as perfect. We know that this approach would be dualistic and futile. It is well to simply keep the Mind stayed on God.

For instance, we know that right here there is Life, Consciousness, Mind, Love. Without considering the individual at all, we hold our Consciousness steadfastly to the Presence of God, who is our own Consciousness and who is the *only* living, conscious Mind in existence.

We are required to love God, so we do love Life, Consciousness, Intelligence, Love. And we know that this Entirety is *all there is of us and all that is here.* In this way, we are not attempting to do something for someone or about a situation. We are not trying to change anyone. Rather, we are "seeing" the *one indivisible Presence which is here,* and this is our own Consciousness, which is our Universe.

If someone should seem to be offensive, selfish, weak, or contrary, we find our Self saying:

> What is that to me? What am I seeing? What am I being? I know what I am; I am what I know. And this is all that concerns me.

Oh, for a little while, we may seem to have to remind our Self again and again of the fact that we have no concern whatever about *any* appearance of evil. But oh, beloved one, we do reach a point where this is no longer necessary. We *are* immune, and we know it.

The Consciousness we really are is Its own immunity to every seeming appearance of evil. Then we find that the seeming situation—as it seemed to be—no longer exists. Either the one, or ones, who seemed to be troublesome move on into another area of activity, or else they no longer even *seem* to be troublesome.

In this case, our Heart always sings because we have "seen" the glory that is God, revealed and evidenced. This is "letting" the Light that we are shine. Thus, we realize the fulfillment of the promise:

> Because thou hast made the Lord, which is my refuge, even the most High, thy habitation; There shall no evil befall thee, neither shall any plague come nigh thy dwelling (Ps. 91:9-10).

Beloved, this is no idle promise. It can be—and is—fulfilled. Have full faith in this fulfillment, and you, too, will see the evidence of its Absolute Truth.

Yes, you remain constant, steadfast, at the very height of the God-Consciousness you know your Self to be. No simulated, fraudulent, evil appearance can even seem to invade the Consciousness that you are—the Consciousness that is your Universe.

"A thousand shall fall at thy side, and ten thousand at thy right hand; but it shall not come nigh thee" (Ps. 91:7). No matter how numerous may seem to be the evidences of illusion, *you remain intact.*

None of these illusions touch you. You are not even aware of their seeming appearances now because you know what you are, and you are what you know.

Now you really know the Absolute Truth, and you know that *you are this Truth Itself, even as this Truth is you.* Now no pseudo so-called person can offend you; no one can annoy or irk you; no one can worry you; and no one can hurt you. Now you know that there is no separate one, and your realization of being the One is glorious indeed.

Now you truly know what it means to be "wise as a serpent, and harmless as a dove." If an occasion arises where you must "speak the word," you speak firmly and decisively. You do not impose, and neither do you permit your Self to be imposed upon. Yet no matter what is necessary for you to say, you know that Love speaks, the Love that is intelligent Principle. In a situation where you must act, you act with firmness and decision. But here, too, you know that it is the Love that is intelligent, principled Love that acts.

Needless to say, no little "I" is around now, and self-righteousness is impossible. You know that every Identity in existence is the very same Consciousness—and equally this Consciousness—that you are. Here you stand, and this stand is unshakable because you know you are on *holy ground.*

Having perceived the fact that eternally and infinitely you are your own immunity to all illusory appearances in and as your daily living, you come to the point of *complete, conscious immunity*. Oh, glorious day—now you know that the Body is as immune as is the Consciousness because the Body *is* your Consciousness. Furthermore, all that you have perceived and seen evidenced in and as your daily affairs is now revealed to be the Truth that is your Body. We know this to be true because we realize that the Consciousness that is aware of Its divine immunity in daily living is the very same Consciousness that is aware of Its immunity as the living Body.

Suppose some illusion of bodily illness does appear to invade the Body. What is that to us? What are we seeing? What are we being? Whatever we are seeing and being, the Body also is perceiving and being. The Consciousness that we are is not aware of a mere illusion. Least of all is this eternal, perfect Consciousness aware of being an illusory, fraudulent, simulated substance. Thus, the Body we are is not aware of an illusion or of being imperfect substance or activity.

> No matter how real or threatening an illusion may seem to be, we are not deceived. We are unshakable because we know that the body remains intact, despite any so-called impositions or appearances of imperfection.

Now, the Body is immune to all appearances of abnormality. This wholly—holy—perfect Body has no awareness of any deceptive appearance that the fraudulent illusion would call malignancy, infection, tumor, inflammation, or of any deception that illusion could present. What is that to you? What is that to the Body that you are? You know what you are. You are what you know. This perfect Body *is* you, knowing what you are. It is you *being* what you know.

In this glorious perception, you are beyond all the pretenses of sickness, and you know nothing of pain. *The body is now immune to pain.* You now perceive the true significance of the statement in Revelation:

> And God shall wipe away all tears from their eyes; and there shall be no more death, neither sorrow, nor crying, neither shall there be any more pain: for the former things are passed away (Rev. 21:4).

Yes, the former illusions are now obliterated, and we now know our Self to be as we have always been and will forever be. Now we remember — are conscious of — the glorious, perfect Being we were and knew our Self to be before the seeming world of illusion began. Now we are aware of being the eternal, changeless, perfect Body we have always known and been.

Here there is no "born" body, no changing or aging body, and no aged body. Here and now there is *only* the everlasting, perfect Body that eternally remains intact, immune to every illusory, fraudulent picture that has ever been or can ever be presented. Indeed, no death is known here. Only the eternal, perfect Body that can never sicken, age, or die is known here and now. All that is known is the perfect Body of God, which is the very God-Consciousness that you eternally and constantly are.

Beloved, *now you know*! Be ever alert. Be ever firm, and you will discover that every word we have spoken is true. You are this Truth, and your Body is this Truth—now, eternally. Your Body is the Kingdom, Consciousness, of Heaven—complete, eternal, perfect harmony, peace, and joy.

You are boundless, immeasurable, eternal, living, conscious, loving Mind. You are infinite; indeed, you are Infinity. You are universal, for you *are* the Universal All. Now you are complete, free from all limitations and restrictions. Now you are beyond simulated birth, age, and death. Now you are beyond all the fallacious restrictions and limitations of an illusory, born being—or body. Now you are beyond all the fallacious laws of sickness, age, pain, or death. Now you are beyond all fear, sorrow, trouble, or anxiety. Now you are beyond all ignorance or darkness, for you *are* all Knowledge. You are the Light. The Light is the Entirety of your Being, and this Light comprises the Body that you are.

Now you know that you are everywhere because you are *the* Everywhere. You know that this Body is but a tiny focal point of the infinite, living, conscious Mind that you are. You know that you are unconfined and uncontained. You know that you could never be confined or contained within the Body. You realize that the Body is as free as is the Consciousness that you are. Freedom, Joy, Peace, and Perfection are omnipresent and omnipotent as the infinite, conscious, living Mind you are.

Beloved, at this point you may find it helpful to ask your Self some searching questions. For instance, "Is it possible that the infinite, living, loving, conscious Mind that I am could ever have been crammed into an infinitesimal pinpoint of the universal, infinite, eternal *I* that I am? Am *I* not eternal, uncontained, and unconfined? How could the infinite, eternal, unconditioned, immutable, Perfection that I am ever know or be an imperfect condition? How could the omnipotent, omnipresent, perfect Omniaction that I am ever act imperfectly?

"Is it possible that this constant, uninterrupted, eternal Omniaction that I am could ever begin? Could It ever end? Could any Substance other than the perfect Consciousness that I am ever live? Is there another substance — consciousness — that can be alive? Is there a living consciousness at all that is not the conscious Life that I am? No!

"Do I not know that I am infinite because I am *Infinitude*? Do I not know that I am eternal because I am *Eternality*? Knowing the infinite, eternal Nature of the Entirety that I am, how could I ever know birth—beginning—or death—ending? Never having been born into, confined, or contained within a pinpoint, how could I ever die out of this pinpoint? How could I ever escape from a prison in which I

Fulfillment of Purpose, Volume Two

was never confined? I know what I am, and I am what I know. This is the only *I* that I am."

You will find that you will ask many questions of the I AM Self that you are. And you will also discover that the answers to all questions you could possibly ask exist right within and *as* your Consciousness. In fact, the perfect answer to every question eternally exists as your Consciousness. This is why the question occurs. If the answer did not exist, it would never occur to you to ask the question. Yes, the very Consciousness that you are is the eternal, infinite answer to every question. It is the *answer* that is first. The question only signifies the Presence of the answer, *and you are this Omnipresence.*

And now, knowing that Everyone in Existence is the same—and equally the same—Consciousness that you are, you can joyously perceive and state the glorious, infinite, eternal, perfect, indivisible, indwelling, all-dwelling I AM Self that you forever are.

Chapter XII

I Am That I Am

I am the Christ that is God, being. I am the God that is the Christ, being. I am "a priest after the order of Melchizedek" (Ps. 110:4). "Without father, without mother, without descent, having neither beginning of days, nor end of life" (Heb. 7:3). This is the Christ I am, for I am that I AM.

I see as I have eternally seen. I know as I have eternally known. I am as I have eternally been, and I am as I will everlastingly be, for I AM THAT I AM. I am completely free from any of the limitations and restrictions of an illusory, temporary "man with breath in his nostrils." I know nothing of birth or death. I am timeless, spaceless, ageless, changeless, living, loving, conscious Mind, knowing *only* the *I* that I am.

I know that I am All, complete within and as my infinite Self. Being constantly, eternally complete, I am the Supply for every seeming need. No matter whether this Supply is evidenced as the Presence of Love, Health, Home, Money, or whatever, *I am aware of being the ever-present Supply for any seeming need.* I know what I am. My perception of the complete Truth that I am this moment is the manifestation I know — and am — right here and right now. I *am* the evidence of the Truth I know. The Presence of the *I* that I am, knowing the Truth that I am, is the manifestation of the Mind that I am, knowing what I am.

The Power of the Presence is the *I* that I am. The Presence of the Power is the *I* that I am. I am the indivisible, indwelling, all-dwelling, omnipotent Omnipresence. I am the Love that is inseparable Oneness. I am the Love that is Perfection, Peace, Joy, and complete Harmony. The Love that I am is the Light that I am. The Light that I am is the Love that I am. Omnipresent, omnipotent, omniactive Love is the *I* that I am.

Beyond creed, beyond all limitations and restrictions, I am. Beyond human motherhood, fatherhood, all relationship, I am. Beyond the pangs of birth and the pains of death, I am. Beyond grief, trouble, change, age, or deterioration, I am. Beyond all pain or suffering, I am. Beyond all the simulated distortions of an illusory world, I am. Beyond the human intellect with all of its delusions, I am. Beyond all conditions, or qualifications, I am. Beyond all sorrow, doubt, frustration, fear, or failure, I am. Beyond all knowledge of the simulated world of egoistic man, I am. All of this I am, for I AM THAT I AM.

I am the fulfillment of the infinite Purpose. I am the fulfillment of the eternal Purpose. I am the fulfillment of the specific Purpose. The infinite Purpose and the specific Purpose are indivisibly *One*. I am the Purpose, and I am the fulfillment of the Purpose. I am the eternal evidence that the infinite—as well as the specific—Purpose in being is eternally fulfilled. I am complete. I am entire. I am here and now the Completeness, the Entirety, that *is* the infinite, eternal Purpose fulfilled as the *I* that I am.

Forever and without interruption,
I AM THAT I AM.

About the Author

During early childhood, Marie S. Watts began questioning: "Why am I? What am I? Where is God? What is God?"

After experiencing her first illumination at seven years of age, her hunger for the answers to these questions became intensified. Although she became a concert pianist, her search for the answers continued, leading her to study all religions, including those of the East.

Finally, ill and unsatisfied, she gave up her profession of music, discarded all books of ancient and modern religions, kept only the Bible, and went into virtual seclusion from the world for some eight years. It was out of the revelations and illuminations she experienced during those years, revelations that were sometimes the very opposite of what she had hitherto believed, that her own healing was realized and that her book *The Ultimate* came.

During all the previous years she had been active in helping others. After *The Ultimate* was published, she devoted herself exclusively to the continuance of the healing work and to lecturing and teaching.

Revelations continued to come to her from within her own consciousness, and they were set forth as she did in this book.

To all seekers for Light, for Truth, for God, for an understanding of their own true Being, this book will serve as a revolutionary but wholly satisfying guide.

Made in the USA
Coppell, TX
13 October 2020